INSIDE OUT, UPSIDE DOWN AND 'ROUND THE RIGHT WAY

Finding Peace in a Crazy Mixed up World

Meredith Resce

INSIDE OUT, UPSIDE DOWN AND 'ROUND THE RIGHT WAY

Finding Peace in a Crazy Mixed up World

Golden Grain Publishing

Personal development; Christian Living

Golden Grain Publishing

P.O. Box 93,
O'Halloran Hill 5158 S.A.

The National Library of Australia Cataloguing-in-Publication information:

Resce, Meredith, 1963-
Inside out, upside down and 'round the right way:
finding peace in a crazy mixed up world

ISBN 0 9585523 8 X

1. Interpersonal relations - Religious aspects - Christianity
2. Christian life. I. Title

248.4

Printed in South Australia by: HYDE PARK PRESS

Cover design and drawings by Daniel Foster ©2001

To the Readers
My prayer is that you find the peace
that every heart yearns for,
and the purpose that comes from
knowing and loving God.

Other Books by **Meredith Resce:**

The *"Heart of Green Valley"* series
Historical romance novels set in colonial Australia

"The Manse"

"Green Valley"

"Through the Valley of Shadows"

"Wallace Hill"

Contemporary Drama:

"A Wretch Like Me - A story of Amazing Grace"
by Meredith Resce

The retelling of the parable of the Prodigal Son, set in modern Australia.

"Picking Up the Pieces"
by Paula Vince

CONTEMPORARY FICTION AT ITS BEST.

About The Author:

MEREDITH RESCE was born and raised in the Southern Flinders Ranges, South Australia, in the community of Melrose.
Meredith met her husband, Nick, when she came to Adelaide to do Bible College in 1981. They were married in 1983, and have three children, Elisa, David and Michael. Together, Meredith and Nick Resce have worked in the ministry for 15 years, having served a six-year period in Geelong, Victoria. They now work with Southside Christian Church, Reynella, South Australia

As well as having completed the Bible College certificate course, she also completed a certificate course in psychology. Apart from writing, Meredith Resce speaks to groups on subjects relevant to the development of relationship skills and growth toward emotional health.

She is actively involved with her 3 children, helping out at their schools, especially in the areas of music and sport.

Acknowledgements:

Thanks to those valuable friends who have worked with me and encouraged me to push through with this project:
Pat Mayfield, Lorraine Evans, Ed Darwood, Daniel Foster, Darren Hunter, Ben Moulton and Peter Heaven.

Thanks again to my husband, Nick, and children, as they continue to support the whole writing, publishing process in this house. One small office, and so many uses!

As always, the Lord Jesus Christ has prompted and pursued this project, as others, and I thank God for His Word and His truth, without which life would not be as full of hope as it is.

“I believe this book takes us a step further in our search for emotional healing. To know that even though people hurt and damage us, we are responsible, by God’s grace to face this issue.
Meredith has ably shared about forgiveness, love and trust in such a way that will facilitate us in our journey to spiritual and emotional health.
I highly recommend this book.”

Mrs Lorraine Evans
Paradise Community Church

INTRODUCTION

It's not what's wrong with the world,
but what's wrong with your heart.

How many times have we heard someone say, or worse yet, said it ourselves, 'I don't know what's wrong with the world!'
I guess every time some drama or crisis has got us in a flat spin, we are tempted to look around for answers. We grasp for something stable to hold on to, and often find that the world seems to be out of control.
Well guess what? The world is out of control. Ever since the time when Adam and Eve chose to disobey God's Word and sin entered the world, things have never been the same! Stuff does happen (actually the bumper sticker uses another word, but we'll run with 'stuff' for the time being). Stuff happens, disaster does lurk around the corner, hurt is inevitable, tragedy waits to strike, and in the finish we all die! That sounds pretty negative, doesn't it? And yet it is part of the reality of this thing we call life, and to ignore the negative doesn't really help us in the long run. But then, for all of those pessimistic 'Hanrahans' out there, we do need to acknowledge the many wonderful things that can be a part of life as well.

Life is an intricately woven tapestry of joys and disappointments, successes and failures, hopes and fears, victories and defeats, better and worse, richer and poorer, sickness and health. And to manage all of these seemingly contrasting experiences, God has given us emotions with which to process these events. We have joy for our triumphs, we have despair for our failures, we have satisfaction for our accomplishments, we have grief for our losses, we have anger for our injustices, and we have happiness for our celebrations.

I have known of young couples preparing for marriage who've wanted to adjust the wedding vows to exclude the negative - worse, poorer, sickness etc - saying that they only want to focus on the positive. I often feel worried when I hear of young people wanting to do this, as it seems that they are buying into the false idea that life is going to be rosy, if only they confess that it should be. Nothing could be further from the truth.

It's not the circumstances about us that govern how much fulfilment we get from life – it's how we respond to the circumstances.

Much of the best part of our character is built during the trying times of life. Our patience is perfected, as it says in James, when we are faced with trial. Something golden is brought from the furnace of grief and suffering. And yet, most normal people wish to flee from those very sorts of trials. Not that I'm wishing for tragedy, it's just that to pretend that we can go through life without it in one form or another, is a huge denial that will eventually land us in a vat full of bitterness.

For one man, blue skies and golden sunshine means peace and contentment, as he faces another beautiful day on the beach as a tourist on holiday. For another, the same blue skies and golden sunshine means gut wrenching despair, as he faces another dry day that adds to the drought that has stricken his land, wasting crops and livestock.

To the owner of a ski-resort, a heavy snowfall means joy as he faces good ski-slopes and more customers. The same snowfall may mean another is lost, and facing the danger of freezing to death
For one man a violent argument and rejection of his religious convictions means despair and worry. To another, who believes that martyrdom is the height of service for his God, it may be an opportunity to further the kingdom of God.

I recall reading the classic story of "Pollyanna" written by Eleanor H. Porter. It is the tale of a little girl who learned early in life to play a game called 'the glad game'. Her father was a minister, and they used to receive a missionary barrel, full of other people's cast-offs that were offered to the minister and his family as a means of support. Pollyanna had expressed over and over her fervent hope that the next missionary barrel would contain a doll.
She had been so hoping for a doll. However, when the barrel arrived, the only thing it contained that was suitable for a child was a small pair of crutches. When her father noticed her utter disappointment, he taught her how to play the 'glad game'. He encouraged her to find something in every situation to be glad about, and started her off by helping her come to the conclusion that she could be glad she didn't need the crutches. From that time on, no matter how dark the situation became, even following the death of her parents, Pollyanna always found something to be glad about.

Whatever happened to Pollyanna?

In our typical western culture, where me, myself and I are the centre of my focus and existence, it is all too common to find a society of people who have absolutely everything - all the bells and whistles and whiz bang gadgets - yet complain constantly about all the woes of life. We have been subtly programmed to expect more and more and more, and expect to give less, suffer less, wait less and serve less. All of these things - giving, suffering, patience and servanthood - are basic characteristics of a follower of Christ, and the promise in return has always been blessing. *Matthew 5:3-12; James 1:2-4*

In the following chapters, I hope to work through a series of thoughts that will encourage an honest look at the way we feel; a courageous recognition of disappointments and hurts of the past; a provoking challenge to accept responsibility for our own failures and mistakes; and a biblical encouragement of just how we can manage in a world that seems bent on overwhelming our senses. I hope to encourage readers to take a thorough look at all the Scriptures that I list, and carefully meditate upon them. I am a firm believer in the power of the Word of God, and have faith that God's Word will work its perfect work in those who choose to meditate upon it. Remember, the Word of God is not rubber - though sometimes it may feel as if it just bounces off your heart. Actually it is sharper than a two edged sword, piercing as far as the division of soul and spirit. *Hebrews 4:12*. Keep applying it to your life, and eventually, you will find that it will break through the hardest of hearts. God Bless you as you take up the challenge to find peace in the midst of chaos.

chapter one

STARTING OUT

Below are listed quite a number of Scriptures that when you have the time to read them through you may feel, as I did when I read them through, that the writers were unnecessarily negative. In fact, some of the listed Scriptures are some of the most negative statements I've ever read, and at one point I felt bad about even quoting them, as they seemed so hopeless and full of despair. But then, I realised that they had been included in the Bible for a reason, and that reason may have been as an encouragement for us.

You see, such famous men of God as King David, King Solomon, Job, and various famous prophets wrote these Scriptures. All of them were supposed to be mighty men of God, and yet these Scriptures show us very clearly that they obviously had days when they felt alone, hurting and in despair.

Please take time to have a read of the following Scriptures:

Ecclesiastes 3:1-8
Ecclesiastes 4:1
Ecclesiastes 12:13
Psalm 22:1-9 (*It is important to note that these words that David cried out in this Psalm were repeated by Jesus Himself, when he hung suffering on the cross. 'My God, why have you forsaken me?' The question we must ask ourselves is, did Jesus really think that God had forsaken Him. Jesus knew the plan of salvation, and knew that the suffering and death on the cross were part of the plan. He knew that he would rise again in victory. I believe that the cry of loneliness, agony and despair came from the depths of Jesus' human self; the part of him that was human, and it was that part that identifies fully with us as human beings. That cry reveals the depths of Jesus empathy for our sometimes traumatic despair. He has been there!*)
Job 3:11
Psalm 139:7-17
Isaiah 40:11-12 and 21 and 27
Psalm 23 (*In this Psalm, the word comfort is the Hebrew word 'nacham', meaning to*

comfort, console, extend compassion, sigh with one who is grieving. It may have originally meant - to breathe intensely because of deep emotion.)
Ezekiel 34:11-12
Psalm 27:10
Habakkuk 1:2-5

What do these Scriptures say to us today, in the new millennium?

Are we always supposed to be 'on top of the world',
'rejoicing in all things',
'looking on the bright side' etc.

Particularly as Christians, there is that added pressure that now that you have the Spirit of God alive in you, you should never feel bad at all. You shouldn't wear a long face, as that is a bad example to others of what it is to be a Christian! And while I'm not suggesting that we fully immerse ourselves in the depths of despair, and accept every invitation to a pity party, I am saying that denial of how we feel is not a particularly helpful practice either.

As has been acknowledged by many professional counsellors -

HURT IS EVIDENCE OF LIFE.

The joy that God gives us now is not to replace suffering and pain, but is there to support us through it.
You may have seen the news story of the child whose nervous system was faulty to the extent that it refused to register pain of any sort. The child simply didn't feel any pain at all. One might have thought this a good thing, until they saw how the child took no precautions against injuring himself, simply because it didn't hurt. He would throw himself off high places, cut himself with sharp objects, place his hand on hot surfaces, and the worst thing I saw was when he dislocated his arm, having tangled it in the spokes of his bike. In all of these accidents he felt no pain, and yet his body was being torn to pieces. Pain is put within us for a reason. It is our signal to be careful, and to withdraw from the battle, as it were. To take time to heal.
The point is, when you lose a loved one, you are supposed to grieve; when you see an outrageous act of injustice you are supposed to feel indignation; when you are betrayed and rejected by close family you are supposed to feel disappointed, anger and loss.

(It is important to note that anger is not actually a sin in itself, as evidenced by the fact that God Himself has and will pour out His anger on unrighteousness. If anger were a sin, then God would not make use of it. Rather, anger is an emotional expression that often is felt as the result of injustice, betrayal, and the like. *Ephesians 4:26-27* actually encourages us to be angry, but warns us not to sin with our anger, as this will give the devil a foothold. How do we sin with our anger? I would suggest if our anger turns to uncontrollable rage where we no longer have control of our speech or action, or if anger motivates us to harm another person either physically or emotionally, then we have crossed over the line into sin.)

The thing we need to sort out is the difference, not necessarily between pleasant and unpleasant emotions, but more importantly, between positive (or constructive) emotions and negative (or destructive) emotions.
God has given each human being an emotional realm as one part of us. It is that part that helps us to experience life to its fullest.
(It must be noted that it is only one of five different parts, and should only be given the appropriate amount of attention, as the emotions will often scream for more, like a tantrum throwing child.)
Perhaps you will have noticed, as I have, that the movies that are the most enjoyable are the ones that move you to an extreme emotion. If you cry really hard, or get fully upset at an injustice, or even laugh really hard, you will often feel as if you have had a fuller experience than a boring old movie that doesn't move you at all. All the frustrating drama and trial that eventually lead to victory is emotionally satisfying in the finish.
However, we often don't want to experience all that drama ourselves.
The fact is, real life deals out emotional drama. It is unavoidable. You will get hurt! (Actually, if you haven't been hurt already, you may want to check whether you are breathing or not).

*As human beings,
we don't like the unpleasant feelings*

But as human beings, we don't like the unpleasant feelings such as the cold, gut-wrenching, sinking feeling that twists our insides into knots. Of course you don't like it! Neither do I! But it is a real feeling nonetheless. When we hear bad news, it is a common feeling. But as humans, we often do just about anything to avoid this kind of feeling. Particularly as descendants of the British, we try to keep the 'stiff-upper-lip', denying ourselves the opportunity of fully entering into the emotions that are associated with loss.

It is common for victims of childhood abuse to have learned early how to push these unpleasant feelings down. Small children seem to have the unconscious ability to deny the pain, and suppress it, and as they grow into adults, having never dealt with it, they continue to deny the old pain, and the new. The trouble is, this very often freezes up the whole emotional realm. There are huge walls built to keep the old pain in, and the new pain out, but they also serve to keep every other emotion out, including joy, happiness and excitement.

This is a very basic analogy, but it really does describe what I'm talking about. In our physical body, God has designed the kidneys, and intestines in such a way that they filter out of our body the toxic wastes. These are eliminated when we use the toilet. If we did not, or would not, go to the toilet, the toxins would build up in our system to the point that they would eventually kill us. Refusing to go to the toilet would be a very bad idea.

Emotionally, we have an elimination system as well. Grieving, sorrowing, and even properly controlled anger are valves through which we eliminate pain, hurt, disappointment, etc. The trouble is, many people have learned to hold on to the past hurts, and refuse to let them pass through the system. Emotionally, these people are killing themselves!

As I said before, the issue is not one of embracing pleasant feelings and denying unpleasant. You see, some pleasant feelings are not necessarily positive or constructive. For example, you may feel happy to see a rival fail in his or her task. You may feel a certain amount of merriment if you are totally full of alcohol. You may get a pleasant jolt of emotion if you partake in a forbidden affair. No one can deny that there are pleasant feelings associated with decidedly negative situations.

The real issue is whether the emotion is constructive or destructive.

If our grief at a loss drives us to the comforting arms of our Father God, where we find peace and healing in our time of pain, then the emotion, though unpleasant, has been constructive. Conversely, if our fulfilment of lust, and the associated ecstasy has driven us to commit adultery, then the pleasant feeling has been decidedly destructive.

You need to analyse your emotions and see where they are leading you before you thoughtlessly abandon yourself to them. If an emotion is leading you on a path

closer to God, then it is constructive. If it is leading away from God, then it is destructive, and should be dealt with carefully.
For the Christian, denial should be carefully monitored. There are certain elements of faith that call for us to deny the difficult circumstances and believe for that which we have prayed for, as outlined in *Hebrew 11:1*. There is plenty of opportunity for that, in a world where things don't always go right, and yet we pray and believe for God to intervene. But this is not a green light for us to deny what needs to be worked through in the emotional realm. Faith is a spiritual exercise, and we need to encourage and build up our faith with positive confession etc. But our emotions need to work as they have been designed to work. The only caution we need to remember with our emotions is, they are there as the icing on the cake, as it were. They are not the masters of our lives. They are the servants. Emotions are like colour and sound at the movie theatre, when years ago it was silent black-and-white.

There are those too-good-to-be-true Christians who never have a down day. Their hair is always straight; they are never ruffled or out of sorts; their common addition to the conversation is, 'Well, praise the Lord'. These people have misunderstood what the emotional realm is all about. They are what I would call plastic Christians. God has instructed us to rejoice with those who rejoice, and to weep with those who weep - *Romans 12:15.* Jesus Himself wept when he saw the grief of his friends at Lazarus' tomb - *John 11:33-37.* Now Jesus understood that He was about to raise Lazarus from the dead. Why didn't He just tell them to all pull themselves together, and settle down?

I believe Jesus understood emotion,
and used it in the appropriate circumstances.

So I guess we can ask ourselves - what good will it do to acknowledge our feelings?

First of all, being honest with ourselves will help to resolve an inner conflict and relieve the problems that result (problems such as compulsive behaviours, obsessive thoughts, stress related diseases).
Secondly, being honest with ourselves is just the start. Then we need to take other steps that will bring us back into right relationship with God, our healer. *Luke 4:18-19; Psalm 147:3*
We could also ask the question - How long will it take for me to get better?

Well, I have to say right from the start - patience is a virtue. There are no microwave answers, short of a lightning bolt miracle. Overcoming hurts of the past and breaking through to spiritual strength and maturity is a little like climbing a mountain. It is of no use sitting at the bottom of the mountain and moaning about how big it is. You had better take your hat in your hand and put one foot in front of the other. Small steps are better than no steps at all. Keep going - even if you have to crawl.

The two following illustrations represent two sorts of Christian: Figure One shows a person who has been brought up in the safety and security of a Christian family. This person has been taught the Word of God, shown the love of God, and has been encouraged to deal with the issues of hurt as they have come his way. At some point in his life he has accepted Jesus Christ as his Saviour and the Holy Spirit as his guide and teacher. The Spirit of God has not only given new life to the spirit of this person, but also permeates throughout his entire being, influencing his thoughts, his emotional realm and the decisions he makes. The fruit of the Spirit, as outlined in *Galatians 5* grows and is expressed in this person's life - attitude and action.

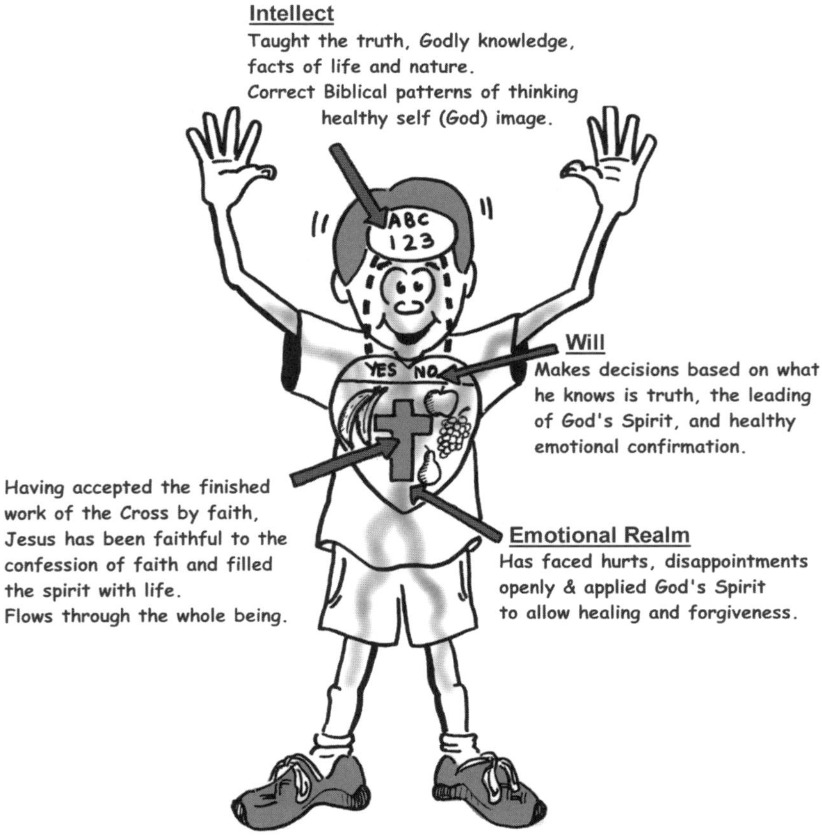

The second illustration is of another Christian person. This man, however, has not had the same safe upbringing of the first character. He has suffered abuse, rejection, and disappointment in a big way. He has not known the Word of God, nor has he known the love of God until his adult years. During his childhood, as each hurt came his way, he carefully constructed a wall around his emotions, the purpose of which was to harden himself against further hurt. He has managed to keep out new hurt, and also to trap old hurt. When he has finally accepted the Lord as Saviour, his spirit has new life, but it is restricted in its access to other parts of the man's life. The emotional realm is frozen, the will is weak, and the mind is full of wrong ideas, perceptions and philosophies. Only over a period of time, as this character submits himself to the working of the Holy Spirit (which will soften the heart), and the Word of God (which acts as a sharp sword and chips away at the hardness) will the bitter contents of the heart be revealed. And then, though it may seem unpleasant, God can actually begin to heal and deal with those past issues.

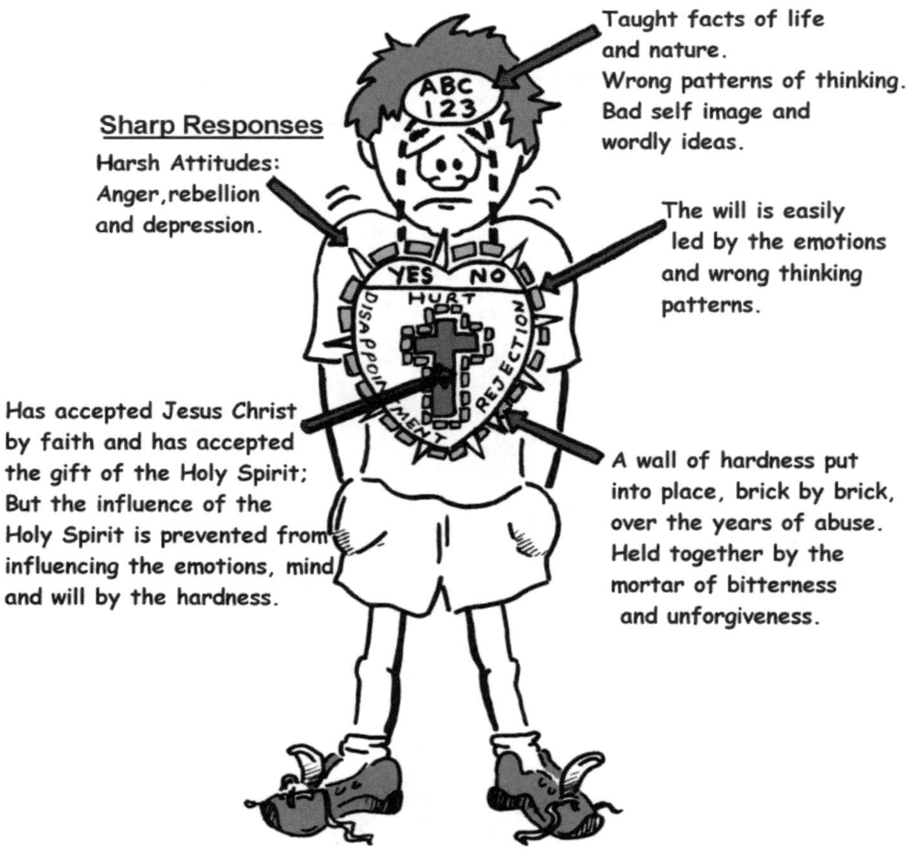

chapter two

LET'S GET REAL!

Acknowledging that which we don't want to acknowledge

There are some things in life that we simply don't want to admit. Of recent times it seems to be a common practice for people to begin to admit that they have suffered some form of abuse or neglect, and the emotional health movement encourages people to openly acknowledge this and deal with some of the accompanying emotions. The acknowledgement of this sort of past trauma is certainly difficult enough, but I believe that there is a whole lot more that needs to be carefully looked at.

How have my legitimate responses crossed over the line and become sin?

In Psalm 51 King David pours out his heart to God in a long lament. It is at that point in his life when he has been faced with his own sin. You may remember that he had committed adultery with his neighbour's wife, and when he found that she was pregnant by him, he orchestrated military events that would ensure that his neighbour was killed. In other words, King David basically had Uriah murdered, after he had stolen his wife. And for a time, King David went on, pretending nothing was amiss. It was only when he came face to face with the prophet Nathan, who seemed to know what David had done, that he realised that his sin had not gone unnoticed, and that it was time to face the fact. Psalm 51 is an expression of his heart at this point in his life.

As you read it through, you will notice several statements:
I admit my shameful deed
You saw it all
You deserve honesty from the heart: yes, utter sincerity and truthfulness
Create in me a clean heart
Restore to me again the joy of your salvation

O my God, you alone can rescue me
A broken and contrite heart, O God, you will not ignore
When my heart is right, then you will rejoice in the good that I do
Make sure you read the whole Psalm.

Here is a strong challenge for us to study our heart in all honesty

John the apostle, in his letter to those under his care, issues the strong lesson, saying that 'if we say we have no sin in us, we are deceiving ourselves'.
1 John 1:8-9
James, in his letter, encourages the reader to admit your faults one to the other.
James 5:16-20
These are all very disturbing thoughts in a time when we generally don't want to be responsible for anything, and looking for someone to blame is the easiest action for any dilemma.
When we are trying to sort out the chaos that exists in our heart, causing all sorts of sicknesses and diseases (emotional and physical) we certainly don't expect that we should have to face the startling truth that any of this could have been our fault!

Now I'm not suggesting that hurts, abuses and traumas inflicted upon a person must always come back to rest at their feet as their own fault. Not at all! Rather, I want to discuss here a few things that we do need to honestly admit.

What is it that we need to honestly admit?

1. First of all, **we need to see that, like every other human being alive, we are in need of salvation.** *Romans 3:23*
There is not one human being ever that has not been in need of salvation from his or her sinful nature. We were all born with it, and we have all lived under its influence. Only the saving power of Jesus Christ's work on the cross, and subsequent resurrection from the dead has brought us freedom from our sins.
2. Secondly, **we must see that there is no hope apart from God.**
All the theories and therapies in the world cannot do what placing my whole life in His hands can do. He made us, He knows how we work, and He knows what it is that is wrong. While psychological science has discovered some principles and practices, only God can truly know what needs to be done to straighten out what has become dysfunctional.

3. Thirdly, **we need to acknowledge that 'wrong has been done to me, and I hurt!'**

Sometimes this is not always easy to admit. Sometimes we feel that such an admission will place us in a highly vulnerable situation, a place where we feel out of control. As human beings, we often have that desperate need to be in control of everything - even the cure of our diseases. But despite this maniacal urge to be in control at all times, the fact is that there are some things that we have to let go of, especially letting go into the hands of our Father God.

Having acknowledged that there is hurt in our life, we then have to examine this next issue:

As a result of that hurt,
I have adopted defence mechanisms and habit patterns.

Psychology has long recognised several unconscious mental practices that they have termed 'defence mechanisms'. One of the most common ones is denial - that state of almost unconsciously denying that the circumstances around about are actually happening. An extreme act of denial is what is called repression. This is a state where a child, unable to face extremely painful circumstances, has totally blocked the memory of the event from their conscious mind. Repression is a total blockage to the point that the adult person simply cannot remember any such circumstance ever happening. In fact, they often cannot remember large parts of their childhood. This is different from **suppression,** where the memory can be recalled if the person allows it.

Other common defence mechanisms are **rationalisation** - where a person subconsciously finds a logical or socially acceptable motive for an unacceptable action. e.g. 'I hit the umpire because he was picking on me!' - a search for an acceptable reason, rather than a true one.

Projection is another defence mechanism where a person who wants to avoid things in their life they don't want to face, simply attributes those bad habits often to other people, usually in exaggerated amounts. If you can convince yourself that everybody cheats on their tax return, then it helps you deal with your own unacknowledged bad habit of cheating on your tax return.

Reaction formation, Intellectualisation and **Displacement** are several other defence mechanisms.

The point is, often, in the midst of pain and trial, one or other of these defence mechanisms comes into play, usually unconsciously, or we could say, naturally. There are a number of bad habits that result from defence mechanisms, bad habits that become life controlling.
The next thing we need to admit is:

Some of those defences and habits have crossed over the line of sin? - therefore I have sinned.

That fact has already been established, but right here, now, in the middle of looking at our past hurts, our own sin doesn't seem to be nearly as bad as what the perpetrator has done to us -does it? Why should I look at my miniscule sins, when their sins are so devastatingly huge?

Let's come back to what John was saying to the people under his care. He says we need to confess our sins! Actually, James said exactly the same thing. And listen to what Jeremiah, the prophet, has to say about the heart of man. "It is more deceitful than all else, and desperately sick! Who can understand it?" *Jeremiah 17:5-10*

The Lord talks about searching the heart and testing the mind.
The bottom line is this: if we really want to sort out the problems that threaten to overwhelm us, we have to be honest, right down to the last little thing. The only place to start is in our own heart, for that is the place where we actually do have a measure of control. Sin in our life is an established reality - let's acknowledge it first up and move on to the next step.

I need to repent

I need to repent! Me? What about them?
Yes, yes! We will deal with them later. But for now, let us repent of our sin.
But how have I sinned? What have I done wrong?
I'm glad you asked!

Overleaf are two lists - the first being legitimate responses to hurt, disappointment, neglect etc, and the second shows how those same responses, when taken too far, cross the line into destructive behavioural patterns (sin)

RESPONSES TO HURT	BECOMES
Anger	Bitterness
Fear	Terrors and phobias
Uncertainty	Insecurity
Feelings of having been betrayed	Loss of trust
Resentment	Hatred
Taking care of oneself	Selfishness and self-centredness
Taking control of the situation	Manipulation and control
Withdrawing from pain	Hardness of heart
Protecting oneself	Emotional shutdown
Cautiousness	Unbelief and scepticism
Sidestepping the pain	Careless abandon
Search for relief	Dependency on temporary distractions e.g. drugs, sexual relationships, the need to be needed
Loss of dignity	Loss of self-respect (an inability to accept that God loves you)
Shame	Guilt and condemnation

In *Jeremiah 18:3-4* the Bible tells us the story about the potter, and his taking the pot, breaking it up completely, and then how he remade it into a new vessel. In *Isaiah 45:9* it asks the question 'does the pot argue with its maker?' Does the pot say 'stop, you're making a really bad job of this', or 'I wish you'd do this another way'.

The point of these two Scriptures is: we are but clay in the hands of our Maker. If it is necessary, He will break a spoiled pot into pieces and start again, and there is little point arguing about it. He is the potter; we are the clay. Best to submit to His superior plan right up front, rather than to fight a futile battle, one that will never achieve anything to our benefit.

Further, in *Jeremiah 17:5-10*, the prophet talks about the difference between the man who trusts in the Lord, and the one who trusts in himself. The basic outcome is simple. Trust in yourself, and you will not make it. Trust in the Lord and you will flourish.

chapter three

FACING THE MUSIC

The difference between conviction and condemnation

In the last chapter we have just looked at some things that need to be acknowledged, not the least of which was the possibility that as human individuals, we may have actually sinned ourselves. Also we may have to come face to face with the fact that we perhaps have been victims of some type of trauma or abuse. Here we can see huge potential for a 'pendulum swing'.

On the one extreme it has been regularly noted that abuse or trauma is the foundational excuse for all of an individual's present bad behaviour. In other words, it is commonly granted that the said individual cannot possibly be held accountable for all of the damage he or she causes to self and others on the account that he or she is a victim.

'Victim mentality' is a popular escape clause from taking responsibility.

It has become very easy, and convenient, to blame anyone and everyone for current failures and mistakes. This tendency, while it may have some basic merit, has run quite wild in its expression, and western society has begun to see its wholesale use amongst the new generations. Damage has been done, and continues to be done, and very few seem to think that they can or indeed should try to stop the flow by taking responsibility for their own actions.

On the other extreme, there is that class of people who in the past have fallen prey to some traumatic event, but quite unlike the 'blamers', they assume that any trouble that has come to them must be of their own making. They have not necessarily enjoyed being the victim of abuse or neglect, but they have concluded that the trauma is their own fault, as is every other dreadful thing that seems to continually dog their lives. They feel as if they are not good enough and that, if there is a God, he is most certainly not willing to give any aid to such as the likes of them.

In the illustration "Living in Extremes" you can see these two attitudes represented on a scale, and also another attitude, somewhere in the middle, that hopefully we can work towards.

Let us look at how we can adopt a balanced attitude towards our current position; the way we are, both as a result of past traumas, and as a result of our own bad decisions and actions. The person in the middle of our scale has adopted this attitude as a starting point: I do hurt as a result of past troubles that have come my way; I have reacted as probably expected, but in all that I have made.some bad choices, and have never properly dealt with the pain and anger.

If I repent, submit to God and learn to forgive, I will get better.

Taking an honest look at ourselves, our feelings and motives is a necessary but risky business; risky because we are always in danger of being tempted to over-indulge in 'self-examination', which has become an overused and destructive pastime. Introspection, as inner examination is often called, should lead us to an honesty that brings us closer to and more dependent on God. Its goal and outcome should reflect a drive towards reaching higher levels of relationship both with God and with others. The trouble is, our old human self is likely to be overcome with the temptation to take a morbid interest in all our sad, sorry past details, and instead of taking them immediately to the feet of Jesus, for His gift of a measure of grace, we may end up bringing them home to use as further material for our campaign for sympathy.

So here we find ourselves; stuck between the one temptation to ignore and deny the past and its associated mistakes and behaviours, and the other temptation to dig up every last sordid detail to add to our résumé of excuses and pleas for leniency.

In the first instance, if denial is our preferred choice of non-action, we continue being totally independent of God, foolishly thinking that we have got the whole thing in control, and moving through life in a continual maze of trial-and-error type of experiences.

But God isn't looking for us to establish ourselves as the self-sufficient, independent unit. He desires our relationship, and our wholeness, and prompts us towards inner honesty. And so the other choice leads us to come face to face with all of that stuff; stuff that often causes a wild panic to surface, as an individual comes face to face with things that they have no control over. As human beings, we hate vulnerability. That is why the 'denial' option is so popular and why the 'reliance on God' option is easy enough to sing in nice church songs, but not so easy to practise in real life.

The 'reliance on God' option is easy enough to sing in nice church songs, but not so easy to practise in real life.

Have you ever watched one of those fishy movies - you know the one where the dolphin makes friends with some sweet-faced child, and then gets sick. The child is determined to find out what has caused his fishy friend to be ill, and invariably, the source of trouble detrimental to our fish is a series of 44-gallon drums that have been secretly dumped in the ocean, at night, by the rich factory owner from just down the road.

The drums have actually been in the water for ages, but it has only been since the metal has started to rust that the toxic waste has begun to seep into our fish-friend's habitat. There is of course an intense scene where the bad factory owner has a stand-off with the sweet-faced child, and the dolphin, of course, knocks the unwary bad guy into his own poisoned waters.

Of course you've seen this kind of movie, and I want you now to picture those drums under the water, the luminous green, poisonous liquid seeping from the barrels into the water. Well, that is how I see past trauma that has been denied. It was originally sealed away in some safe sort of barrel, and then dumped in the outer recesses of the subconscious, and a sign warning of piranhas was posted to prevent further investigation. Now an individual can continue along many years, merrily ignoring the toxins of the past, but eventually, the barrels begin to disintegrate, and the stuff will seep into everyday life.

Another analogy, more modern in its concept, is that of the hard drive on your computer. Now I don't know a lot about computers, but I have seen warning notices about hard drives being low on virtual memory (whatever that means) and also notices that say that the floppy disc has no more room to store any more information. I believe our subconscious is a bit like a floppy disc. It can store away lots and lots of emotional stuff, positive and negative, but eventually, a sign will come up in a person's life that says 'sorry, there is no more disc space. You are going to have to deal with this one!' Our emotional disc space was never meant to just save stuff, and save more stuff. I believe it was only ever designed as a temporary storage, a place from where it can be recalled to deal with at a time that is safe and secure. The most safe and secure time to deal with any emotional issue is when you are fully centred in the middle of God's all - consuming love.

Ok, so I assume that perhaps you are ready to accept that continual denial is not necessarily healthy, and neither is the morbid, negative introspection that is self-centred rather than God-centred.

We need to be careful to balance the scales between EXCUSE and REASON

❊ Things of the past that have hurt us may be honestly acknowledged and evaluated, always tending towards bringing things to God's healing heart, rather than accumulating them for our own attention-seeking case for trial.

❊ Being a victim of any sort of abuse is often a legitimate *reason* why our lives have become tangled and out of control.

❊ Being a victim of any sort of abuse ***is not*** an ***excuse*** for sin.

❊ Ignorance sometimes allows us to form bad habit patterns (sin) without realising it.

❊ Sin fosters and breeds further destruction in our lives.

❊ When we finally come to face the music, we may feel the grief, sorrow, pain and anger, but we must also see our own responses clearly, and become responsible for them.

❊ We need to repent of sin - the result of badly informed choices - to take away the enemy's legal right to accuse us. Our enemy, the devil, will look for any and every opportunity to bring our sin to fling in our face continually. He wishes us to remain bowed under the burden of guilt and shame - condemnation.
Read *Romans 8:1-4*

❊ Repentance of sin and confession of belief in Jesus Christ as our Saviour results in righteousness (this is not self-righteousness, but right standing in God's eyes) Read *Romans 10:9-10 and Romans 5:1-2,5*

❊ If we are used to bad habits, we now need to look continually to our new counsellor, the Holy Spirit, who leads, guides and shows us into all truth. This will result in constant emotional and spiritual growth. *Read Romans 7:15-25; Galatians 5:1; Galatians 5:16-26 these Scriptures are expressed very clearly in the Living Bible translation.* The Apostle Paul is quite clear in expressing his frustrations in *Romans 7,* about how he seems to be always doing the things he knows are wrong, and the very things he knows are right, and wants to do, he fails to achieve, even to doing the opposite. Read this Scripture. It will encourage you, if you think you need to be perfect right away.

❊ Failing and falling down does not mean we have blown our one and only opportunity. We are babies at this, and God gives us time to get up and try again. He has far more time for us than we give ourselves.

❊ God wants us to be aware of sin, and to repent of it. He does not, however, want us to be pounded into the ground with feelings of unworthiness, condemnation and guilt. *Read 2 Corinthians 7:9,10* We need to be able to tell the difference between the sorrow that Paul rejoices in - the kind that leads a person to repentance and restoration with God called conviction - and the sorrow of the world that produces death (condemnation). That kind of deep, mind-tormenting despair is the kind that drives a person away from the loving arms of God, and further into self-rebuke, remorse and self-punishment. The punishment for all our sins has been paid for already, through the death of Jesus Christ on the cross. The freedom from sin has been made available to us the moment Jesus rose from the dead, victorious over sin and death. *1 Corinthians 15:54-57.* Once we have accepted this truth, and have committed ourselves to living the way Jesus, our Lord and Saviour, has directed us to, we don't have to live under the mental pressure that accusation and condemnation so often brings. That doesn't mean we may not be tempted to think in the old pattern, but it does mean that when those sorts of condemning thoughts cross our mind, we can challenge them with the truth.

Read *Romans 6:15-23; John 8:31-32*

Some of these life-changing steps may seem huge at first, maybe even impossible. Letting go of the controls can sometimes seem like a mad and crazy thing to do, especially in a world where we are carefully programmed to take control all the time. But there are some situations that need to be released, and dealing with emotional issues and related sin are such situations.
The issue of learning to trust God to handle these without our help may be something we need to look at later. Always remember, the Holy Spirit will convict us of sin, if we listen to his conscience-like prodding. But it is not the Holy Spirit that lays condemnation and guilt upon us. Those feelings of utter unworthiness and hopelessness have their origins from the devil himself, and must be challenged everytime.

Read *Revelation 12:9-11*

chapter four

THE LAST FRONTIER

Winning the Battle of the Mind

Having talked about acknowledging things in our life, and taking dramatic action to set some things into right order, there are several things to be noted. First of all, perhaps it would be good to recognise the different parts of what makes up a whole person.

A whole person is made up of a spirit, soul and body.

The body is the obvious part of us that we are all familiar with, and are all very used to taking care of. We feed, clothe it, clean, and pamper it as much as we can.

Another part of us is our spirit, which we have been making reference to. Our spirit is that part of us that, when we were born physically, was not alive. It was dead to God and bound under the curse of sin. But when we confess Jesus Christ as our Lord and Saviour and believe in our hearts, our spirit comes alive in Him. *Ephesians 2:1-10; 2Corinthians 5:16-21; Romans 5:12-19; Colossians 2:13; 1 Peter 3:18; 1 Corinthians 15:20-23 This Scripture reads very clearly in the Living Bible translation.* In the scripture Paul tells us how through the disobedience of one man, Adam, all mankind came under the curse of death, but through one man's obedience, Jesus Christ's act of sacrifice, that curse has been broken, and eternal spiritual life has been won. Now our spirit can be given life. *Galatians 2:20* Paul tells us that it is no longer we who live, but Christ who lives in us.

The soul is made up of three parts: the mind, the emotions and the will.

The other part of us the Bible refers to as our soul or heart, and is actually made up of three working parts: The emotions, which we have already been discussing; the will, which really is the part of us that has the power to make decisions; and the mind. What can we say about the mind? Psychology has spent many many years trying to figure out just how our mind works, but in the finish, who can really know? The prophet Jeremiah writes of the heart that it is more deceitful than anything else, and he says that it is 'desperately sick'. He says of the heart, 'who can understand it?' *Jeremiah 17:9*

It is really hard to define where the mind ends and the emotions begin, or where the emotions end and the will begins. The three components seem to be intricately entwined, and each directly influences the other. The thing is, the Spirit of God, once living in our now alive spirit, can and should also begin to influence each of these mysterious realms.

The funny thing is, or perhaps it really isn't so funny, the emotions are not supposed to actually rule our lives, and yet, as I said earlier, they seem to be able to put on such a colourful display of temper that we often yield to their tantrums. Why is it so? Is it perhaps that our mind is in a state of disorder and indiscipline? Has our will become so used to following along, like a meek, henpecked husband, and allowing all sorts of crazy decisions to be made simply because somewhere in ourselves, we don't really believe we have the ability to stand up against the overwhelming emotional tides that seem to swamp us.

Let us look at the mind and the will, and the things that we can do to improve the discipline required to bring about a little order in our lives. Our emotions probably won't like it very much, and will typically pout or scream. But, hey! Who's really in charge here?

Our mind is really the last untamed frontier. Once the spirit has been yielded to the saving power of Jesus Christ, it is saved. What happens in our emotions can only get out of control if our will allows it. But our mind is like an open forum. Our eyes see, our ears hear, and our other senses feed us information as well. Add to this the huge backlog of information that has been stored away in our memory, and there are hundreds of thousands of thoughts, ideas and impressions that can come to mind every day.

There is the wise rule that you can employ to protect your mind from destructive input - obvious ones being things like pornographic images, horror inspired tales and pictures, disgusting depraved talk etc. Now while you can take up an active campaign to try to protect yourself from such negative input, there are still past memories that are easily recalled, and usually at the most inconvenient times. What is a person supposed to do about these?

Unfortunately, in this high tech society, with the fast paced information highway, there are literally thousands upon thousands of negative images and bits of information that have already been registered in your subconscious. This makes the job of winning the battle of the mind a little more difficult, but still, it can, and must be done.
The point is this:

The mind is a battleground, and we must fight to take control

There are a number of things that are what we would call 'classic strongholds' (points where we have little or no control). Examples are:

- Fear
- Depression
- Lust
- Uncontrollable anger (rage)
- Inferiority
- Chemical dependency (e.g. alcoholism, drug addiction)
- Sexual addiction
- Need to manipulate and control
- Image disorders (anorexia, bulimia)

There are probably many other different kinds of strongholds of the mind, but these are common ones. Now if these strongholds have been lifelong and practised, they may also have become spiritual strongholds, and need to be broken by the power of the Holy Spirit in Jesus' name. But once this is done, there is still the mind battle to deal with. Unlike the computer hard drive, we cannot delete the negative information and bad memories. All we need is some sort of trigger to relate to a certain stronghold, and those thoughts come flooding to mind. If the emotions have an issue, they start their little song-and-dance routine, and the will hardly stands a chance of taking the matter in hand. That is when a Christian individual gets very discouraged because they find themselves in the middle of some familiar negative behaviour that they had no intention of ever doing again.
One thing is for certain, our will is going to have to develop some backbone, and learn to stand up in the middle of all the mental and emotional turmoil. Our will is going to have to make some strong decisions based upon the truth of the Word of God, and not upon how we feel or the whirling chaos of thoughts that seem to have besieged our intelligence.

At these moments in life, you need to keep handy the following Scriptures for quick and easy reference.
Romans 12:2 Paul urges the Romans to be transformed by the renewing of their mind.
1 Peter1: 13-14 encourages us to gird up our minds for action and keep sober in spirit.
Ephesians 4:17-25 tells us to get out of the futility of the mind that had been darkened in ignorance and hardness of heart, and again encourages us to be renewed in the spirit of our minds.
Ephesians 5:1-17 Paul encourages the Ephesians with a list of directives about how to live, including watching out for negative, coarse talk, keeping guard against immorality and greed, and unfruitful deeds of darkness. He ends his exhortation by telling them that they must understand what the will of the Lord is and to be wise.
2 Corinthians 10:4-5 speaks of fighting, not with natural weapons, but with the Spirit, and taking captive every thought, and bringing it into obedience to Christ.
Philippians 4:6-7 talks about the peace of God guarding our hearts and minds, through Christ Jesus.
Colossians 3:1-2 encourages us to set our minds on things above, rather than things on earth.

As always, I strongly encourage you to read the full Scriptures set out above, and even better, begin to commit some of them to memory.

*I like to think of my spiritual/inner self as a family. The **will** really is the head of the house, and by rights has the authority and power to make good, positive decisions. Those decisions are the basis upon which we act, and our **body** becomes the servant to outwork those decisions, either in action or speech. Ideally, our will should make those decisions based upon relevant Biblical information and spiritual guidance from the Holy Spirit within us, and the final outcome should yield the right sort of **emotions** to help us enjoy the satisfaction of a job well done, or a word well spoken. The trouble is, the **emotions**, are is really the member of the family in charge of all family celebrations and formal occasions, has got out of control. When the emotions should be hanging the streamers and blowing up the balloons for the celebration of joy, or alternatively, should be arranging the formal wake in honour and respect of a loss, it is often found running about the family home screaming for attention, demanding its own way, sulking, manipulating and generally making chaos for everybody else. If our family **intelligence** has been out in the world, partaking of all the nonsense that the world has to offer, and has not been studying the Word of God as the scholar of*

the family should, it will probably not have any concrete advice to give to the head of the house, the will. Instead, it may undermine the head's authority by reciting all sorts of worldly ideas like 'perhaps we should just let the emotions have their own way, dear!'; 'We shouldn't really try to stop them from having a good time'.
If this sounds a little like your inner family, then perhaps you need to start to give the ***will*** *a bit of help. You need to know that, despite any wrong ideas your* ***mind*** *has previously absorbed, and despite the wild feelings your* ***emotions*** *throw at you, your* ***will*** *is still the control centre of your being. You can actually make decisions based upon the truth of the Word of God, even in the face of strong opposition. Ask yourself the questions: where has all of my impulsive, emotionally charged decisions gotten me in the past? Could I have made better decisions if I had simply told my emotions to go and sit in the corner for a time, while I thought the situation through properly?*

Below are some helpful steps towards challenging the pattern of wrong thoughts, and establishing new patterns of thought:

❇ Know who you are in God by developing a relationship with God. This can be achieved by reading the Word of God, also by sitting in classes or meetings where the Word of God is taught.

❇ Read and meditate (think over continually) on the Word of God. Read *Deuteronomy 6:6-9; Joshua 1:8* (Always pray before you read, that the Holy Spirit will show you God's heart from the Scriptures)

❇ See yourself as different and new, taking to the task of renewing your mind daily. Read *Ephesians 4:23-25; 2Corinthians 5:17* Paul tells us that if we are in Christ we are a new creation, and that the old things have passed away. We need to start to believe this.

❇ Act in line with God's Word. There is the way that you have perhaps been used to, and if this is in contrast to what the Word of God says, then you need to act differently. Read *James 1:22-25* Don't just hear the Word, you need to decide to do it. Now here we recognise where the battle will really begin, as your emotions will resist, either through laziness, selfishness or stubbornness. They will tempt you to ignore what you have heard, and your mind may begin to process past thought patterns to add some weight to this temptation. At this point you need to actually stand up and shout, **"STOP!"** Remember it is your will that has the power to make the choices. At this point of temptation talk to God, or even a trusted counsellor, and admit the wrong thoughts, asking God to forgive you.

Then deliberately choose an opposite thought to dwell on. Deliberately and methodically begin to go over the opposite in your mind. If you are attacked with fear, immediately begin to think about faith, if not your own, then think of some heroes of faith, either from the Bible, or even from modern day testimony. Think about their obedience in faith, and begin to think the stories through. Fear and faith cannot occupy the same mind at the same time. If it is lust that has attacked your mind, then immediately admit it to God, ask for his forgiveness and start to think on things opposite. Singing songs of praise that you may have learned from church, or quoting Scripture is equally good, if you simply can't get any positive things to think on. Remember, you really can only think on one thing at a time. Read *Philippians 4:8*

❊ Now, more than ever, act upon what you know is right. Make it a deliberate, almost defiant stand against the stronghold, firmly committed to challenging the wrong thoughts that have come into your mind.

Winning the battle of the mind is not an instant or quick cure. In fact, the mind is open for attack for the rest of your earthly life. However, the more you practise taking authority over wrong thinking, and practise acting on the truth, the stronger you will grow, the more you will succeed in winning, and the less attacks you will endure. Don't ever come under condemnation because revolting, wrong thoughts cross your mind. That happens as a result of the material that has been flung carelessly about through our popular media.

A bird can come and sit on your head,
but you don't have to let it build a nest there.

A disgusting thought is just that, disgusting, but it is not a reason to come under guilt unless you allow it a bit of airtime. It is only if you allow the thought to stay, think on it a bit, indulge in the lust of it a bit, that it can feed a weakness or stronghold in your life. If you immediately resist it and tell it to get lost, you have done a good thing.

chapter five

FORGIVENESS

That really scary word

Now that we have discussed being honest, taking responsibility for our actions, and taking control of our thought life, it is time to face that next big challenge in our life: that of forgiving those that have hurt us in the past.
Now I can just imagine all sorts of wild reactions: fire erupting from nostrils and steam coming from ears. When I've mentioned this word in the past, many times I've had those kinds of reactions.
'Why should I forgive?' 'That sort of person doesn't deserve to be forgiven!' 'I can't let him off the hook, just like that!'

At this point, I would like to drop in a little commercial. I have written several novels, and would like to recommend one of them to you. The story "Through the Valley of Shadows" puts into dramatic context this whole issue of forgiveness, where my main character, Christine Shore, faces the fact that she is going to have to forgive the man who has raped her. Believe me, her reaction to the concept of forgiveness was so overwhelming that even I began to wonder if she would ever be able to get over it.

You see, it wasn't hard for me to create Christine's character, her personality or her reactions in this horrible situation, because I have sat with many real-life people over the years, and the reaction is nearly always the same: one of absolute horror at the very idea.

Now I am not going to glibly tell you that forgiveness is as easy as one, two, three, because I know that it's not! But I am going to tell you that holding onto the bitterness and resentment associated with unforgiveness will only ever destroy one person - you!

Holding on to the bitterness and resentment of unforgiveness will only ever destroy one person – you!

The perpetrator, whom you are holding so bitterly in your subconscious thoughts, doesn't even have any idea how badly you feel about him or her, and in some cases probably doesn't even care.
But don't let me get ahead of myself.
Let me start right at the beginning by looking at the whole definition and meaning of the word forgiveness.
Webster's dictionary defines forgiveness as: ***the act of forgiving; the pardon of an offender, by which he is considered and treated as not guilty***.
This definition is the generally acknowledged meaning of the word forgiveness, but if we look at the original words used in different Scriptures, both the Hebrew and the Greek, we may see another meaning also.

In the Scripture *Mark2:7* '...who can **forgive** sins but God alone?' the Hebrew word Salach (saw lakh) which means to forgive, pardon, spare; is the same definition that Webster has used.
In the Scripture *Luke 6:37* '...Forgive and you will be forgiven', it is from the Greek word apoluo (ap-ol-oo-o) which means to relieve, release, dismiss, forgive, let go, loose.
When considering forgiveness, it is important to note that it is only God Himself who can pardon us from sin, and allow us to escape the punishment due to us for our wrong doing. In other words, God, in that kind of forgiveness, views us as if we have never done anything wrong in the first place. This of course was the result of the work done through the death and resurrection of Jesus Christ, and is accepted by faith by each individual.
However, we are continually encouraged to forgive others, and in this case, it is to release others from the resentment and bitterness we hold against them; to let them loose. In the long run, the most benefit from this act is for the forgiver, as much as it is for the forgiven party.

Let me illustrate: Suppose I was to walk through the crowded church foyer one day. On this particular occasion, I was in somewhat of a hurry, and was in search of someone who needed my urgent attention. As I was bumping and excusing my way through the crowd, I happened to walk straight past you, not even seeing you in my state of distraction. Unfortunately, because of this preoccupation and my failure to notice you, my walking straight past seemed to be a deliberate slight, and I pushed past, continuing on my merry way.

However, you were unaware of my thoughts and intentions, and your immediate interpretation was that this was an intentional attempt to offend, that I have gone out of my way to ignore you. As a result, you feel angered and begin to express your disappointment and hurt to others. It isn't too long before you decide that you will not be making any contact with someone as rude as I am, and the relationship is closed down from your end.
During all of these mental and emotional deliberations, I remain blissfully unaware of the offence, though it isn't too long before I begin to sense that something is amiss. Probably those daggers floating through the air give me a clue. I try to reopen the lines of communication, but my attempts are met with 'the cold shoulder' treatment. I am now in a place where I can no longer share anything with you, no matter what I try to do. In your eyes, I have deliberately hurt you. Resentment will most assuredly build, and before long, bitterness will begin to eat away at your emotional well-being. If this problem continues unchecked, hatred may also eventually take a foothold. All three of these emotions have crossed the line from acceptable response into sin, and each will exact the price required from your emotional well-being.
I use this illustration specifically when I talk about the need to examine our relationship with God. There are many instances where people knowingly, or unknowingly, are angry and bitter at God. To begin the whole forgiveness program, I believe that an individual must first reopen the lines of communication with their God and Maker. Many people feel that God has let them down at a time when they most needed Him. They feel angry and hurt, and they blame God, closing down the lines of communication, and allowing resentment and bitterness to grow in their lives. It is not until they realise that God has not done them wrong, but rather it has been perceived by them as His having done wrong, and they choose to release, let go (apoluo) of their resentment and anger, that anything can be achieved. In this instance, a person cannot forgive (Salach) God, as in pardon or overlook his sin, because God has not sinned. But they can release (apoluo) their own resentment toward Him and turn back to Him, thus reopening the lines of communication and blessing.

This is the first point of forgiveness in every life.
Perhaps you may not yet be convinced that forgiveness is anything other than a kind suggestion for your benefit. Well, it is for your benefit, that is true, but as to a kind suggestion, it is far more than that. Let's do a quick investigation of what the Bible has to say on the subject of forgiveness.

In *Mark 11:24-25* Jesus says it right out. If you don't forgive, neither will your Father who is in heaven forgive you. He makes a point that you should forgive anything against anyone at the point where you have come to ask for things in prayer.

In *Matthew 18:21-35* Peter asks Jesus just how many times we are meant to forgive. Jesus answered using a parable of a man who owed a lot of money, and begged that his lender would forgive him his debt, as he didn't have the money to pay. When he was forgiven he then went straight out to another man who owed him a small amount, and when this man begged him for the same forgiveness, he refused and threw the borrower into prison. When the first master heard about it, he was angry at this man's unforgiving attitude, when he had been forgiven so much. Jesus indicates from this parable that the anger of God will burn against those Christians who have received the life-giving forgiveness of God and yet who refuse to forgive other people.

In *Ephesians 4:31-32* Paul is encouraging the Ephesian Christians to put away bitterness, wrath, anger, slander and malice, instead to be kind, tender-hearted and forgiving of one another. He reminds them that it is just as God, in Christ has forgiven us.

In *1 Peter 3:8-9* Peter writes to those under his care, giving encouragement to be harmonious, kind-hearted and humble in spirit, and then adds the counsel that they should not return evil for evil, but give a blessing instead.
In Luke 6:27 Jesus, once again, commands His followers to love their enemies, do good to those that hate them, bless those who curse them and harder yet, to pray for those who have mistreated them. He points out very clearly that it's of little account to only do good to those who do good to you. He makes the point that even the sinners do this much.

In *Romans 12:17-21* Paul also teaches the Roman Christians not to pay back evil for evil to anyone. He says, that if it is at all within your power, be at peace with everyone, in other words, deal with whatever issues you can. He gives the charge never to take your own revenge, but to leave room for the wrath of God. He quotes an Old Testament Scripture, words of Almighty God, 'Vengeance is Mine, I will repay'. Paul also encourages this group of believers to feed their enemy, if he is hungry.
Hebrews 10:26-36 holds a very stern warning for those who have known the truth of forgiveness, but have deliberately turned their back on God, taking his cleansing blood and forgiveness and treated it as common. The writer of Hebrews is very solemn in his caution, saying that it is a fearful thing to fall into the hands of the living God. He also quotes, 'Justice belongs to me; I will repay,' says the Lord. The issue of forgiveness is not necessarily popular in a self-oriented society. Human nature's own warped sense of justice often wants

to exact its own payment for wrongs done. However, Scripture is more than clear that this is not the way at all. We can conclude from the above Scriptures that forgiveness is a command, not just a nice suggestion, and that to ignore this command brings dire consequences. Better go and have a look at those Scriptures again!

We must not forgive too quickly

What on earth do I mean by forgiving too quickly?
Sometimes, when a person has heard all of the Scripture and teaching on the evils of unforgiveness, they may, without properly considering everything, spout out an insincere prayer, and an equally shallow confession of having forgiven someone. However, we must be careful at this point because often all that is achieved is a denial of the truth; the truth being that they are still full of anger and resentment. But now they have buried this barrel full of bitter trouble under a thin blanket of insincerity, pushing it to the outer recesses of their consciousness, never to be looked at again. And in its place they put on a spiritual façade. They then begin living a pretence, all the while allowing bitterness and unforgiveness to continue its evil in the subconscious.

We must lay a foundation for forgiveness

After all the sermons have been heard, a wise counsellor should encourage a person to start the program of forgiveness as soon as is possible. The program must start with the laying of a foundation.

First, it is good to realise that forgiveness is not an attribute that can be retrieved from our so-called 'good nature'. Real forgiveness is something that God plants in our lives, and as we water and encourage its growth, we will reap the fruit.
A good first step towards forgiveness is praying, 'Lord, help me to want to forgive!'

'Lord, help me to want to forgive!'

The honest analysis of any situation is that our human nature does not particularly want to forgive. If we find it easy to forgive, then perhaps we have not really been hurt, or God has already been preparing you in a way that forgiveness is ripe and ready to use.One of the major obstacles to forgiveness is the idea that many people have, that to forgive means one has to trust an abuser or perpetrator again. For this reason, many struggle and fight against the very concept of forgiveness. But this is not the case.

Forgiveness and trust are two different issues.

Forgiveness is clearly a commandment, and it has been observed that it is to the health and benefit of the forgiver. Trust, on the other hand, is something that must be earned; that is in reference to other people. Where God is concerned, full trust in God is for our health and benefit also, but learning to trust God is not so much His having to earn it from us, more than us having to learn to master the art of trusting Him.

We will discuss the issue of trust in another chapter.

Where trust has been betrayed, it must be regained applying much wisdom and time. A relationship may never regain full trust again. This is a consequence of sin.

Where manipulative actions and selfishness have caused havoc in a relationship, new ground rules and boundaries should be discussed and applied.

The forgiveness program and the trust program are both developed over a period of time, and in conjunction with a growing relationship with God. To finally be free from resentment, hatred, bitterness and unreasonable anger is a relief from a heavy and destructive burden. Where, over time, relationships can be healed by the rebuilding of trust and responsibility, restoration and reconciliation may take place. If done properly, this is always a blessing.

Sadly, not all parties can be reconciled, simply because there are some parties who are not willing to pay the price of being responsible and trustworthy.

In these cases, the best we can work towards is the freedom from resentment and bitterness over the broken relationship and related events.

Where outrageous betrayal or abuse have been the cause of our unforgiveness, we must examine our feelings constantly. It is easy to allow our anger and/or fear to lead us down many and varied roads of sin. Even after we have started along the road to forgiveness, a reminder of the incident may cause all those old emotions to come flooding back with a force. It is at these times that we must choose to renew our prayer and confessions. If we keep taking a positive stand against the temptation to lapse into bitterness each time the temptation arises, then eventually those times will become less frequent and less harsh. Jesus said we must forgive seventy times seven. *Matthew 18:21-22* This may mean to forgive the same person for seventy times seven different offences, but it could also mean that we can forgive the same person of the same offence the same number of times, each time the memory of that offence causes wrong feelings to well up inside.

chapter six

LEARNING TO TRUST

In the face of past betrayal

As I stated very clearly in the previous chapter, forgiveness and trust are two totally separate issues, and each needs to be examined individually.
Just because you need to release the bitterness and anger you hold towards a serial killer, doesn't mean that we should immediately say, 'There, there! Now that I have forgiven you, I must let you out on the streets again.
I have to trust you.'

I would like to ask the question of where in the Bible it says that we must trust those who have severely abused our trust in the past. In Matthew 7:6 Jesus tells us not to give what is holy to dogs, and further, not to throw our pearls (precious, valuable possessions) before pigs, because he warns that they will trample them under their muddy, ungrateful feet, and they could very well turn on you and tear you to pieces.

I see trust as something very precious and valuable. As far as I am concerned, I treat the trust that other people have in me as something that needs my utmost care. I know that I am not one hundred percent perfect in taking care of that trust, but I certainly take the charge seriously.
And conversely, if I should extend trust to another person, it is only as much as I can afford to lose. By that I mean, if the other person does not have a good record - for example, my husband's record of posting letters is not good - I do not trust them with something important. If I have an important letter to post, one that I simply can't afford to have posted late, I will not give it to my husband at all. I cannot afford the risk of him not posting it. He might post it, and then again, and more likely, he will forget to post it. I simply cannot trust him in this. If the letter is not really important, like some answer to a Reader's Digest contest, I can afford to lose that for all time, and therefore will take the risk of asking him to post it. There is always the chance that he will succeed.

Let's consider Noah Webster's dictionary definition of the word 'trust'. In the context of which I am talking it means:

Confidence; a reliance or resting of the mind on the integrity, habitual truth, justice, friendship or other sound principle of another person.

When you really consider all of those qualities in reference to another person, even someone you know very well - even the minister of your church, you would have to agree with me that your confidence would have to be on a shaky foundation.

The fact is there is not a human being alive who can be trusted 100% on every occasion.

When we are talking about a resting of the mind (that sounds very trusting) on the integrity, habitual truth, justice or friendship of someone else, there is only one person or being who could fit this category, and unfortunately, it isn't me! Obviously I am referring to Almighty God, creator of the universe, Lord of heaven and earth, Saviour of the World. There is no one else who could be one hundred percent trustworthy all the time.

Jeremiah 17:5-10 puts it very clearly. It says that if you put your trust in man, his ways and his strength, you will be like a bush or a tree that is planted in the desert. When the trials of life come along, you will find that there is nothing in your man-placed confidence to sustain your life. You will wither and die. On the other hand, Jeremiah says that if you put all your confidence and trust in the Lord, and make the Lord your hope, you will be like a tree situated right next to a river. When those same trials and storms of life come your way, your leaves will remain green, and you will continue to bear fruit, and the reason will be because your source of trust is unfailing.

The Apostle Paul knew about this kind of trust in the Lord. In *2 Timothy 1:12b* he uses really strong words like 'convinced', and 'believed', when he refers to that which he has 'entrusted' to God's guard. He talks about the trustworthiness of the One on whom he has staked his faith.

And let's face it; if we are going to put our faith in someone, there is no point unless we can believe that they are unfailing in their trustworthiness. I don't know of any man or man-made organisation that I would have confidence enough in to stake my life upon it. God and His Word is the only thing that I believe is wholly unshakeable.

To some people the word 'trust' equals vulnerability, and that equals utter terror.

To be vulnerable, the dictionary states, is to be in a position whereby you could be wounded. In other words, you are liable to injury. And any person who has been hurt or abused in the past knows all about vulnerability, and just how much they don't intend to be in that position again.

The trouble is, when a person, reacting to past hurt, takes up the reins of control, determined that they will never be open to injury of any type ever again, it makes for a very hard person. Not only that, the absolute terror of vulnerability, and the obsessive need to be in control can help create a personality that is what is often referred to as a 'control freak'; one of those people who manipulate any way they know how, either by using temper, emotional blackmail, insensitive strength of will, or any other bull-dozing tactic that gets the job done.

You may have been the object of someone's manipulation before, or, more than likely, you have practised it yourself (we probably all have at one time or another). But being in control at all times, arranging and organising every tiny detail in your life, and the lives of those around you, makes it very difficult for you to trust God. You see, there are times in every life where you just have to let go of some things - let them go into God's safe hands, and you can't do that until you've dealt with the issue of control; that is to say, until you've dealt with the issue of trusting God. Perhaps you need to re-read the portion in the previous chapter about forgiving God, and reopening the lines of communication with Him.

I would like to share two different analogies with you:
Consider a small child who sees a cuddly dog for the first time, and is overwhelmed with a desire to pat it. If that dog savagely mauls this child, she will more than likely develop a fear of dogs. The reasoning behind this fear is obviously that if a dog has bitten her once, it will most assuredly happen again. She does not know any other option where dogs are concerned. Suppose, in her adult years, she has a friend come to her door, bringing a large cuddly dog along. The friend suggests that she take the dog into her home as a companion, friend and protector. It is unlikely that this woman will respond positively to this suggestion. All of the old fear will surface, and the memory of that childhood attack will possibly dictate her frame of mind. If, however, her friend reassures her that this dog is different, and that he can be trusted, it will make little difference to the way the woman emotionally feels about dogs, though she

may take her friend's word, and accept the dog. Still, the relationship between woman and dog will be strained and suspicious until, bit-by-bit, the dog proves that it may be trusted as a friend and protector. At first the woman might keep the dog on a leash, locked away in the laundry, and might hurriedly throw the dog food in through the laundry door. After a time, when the woman notices that the dog doesn't leap viciously at the door, barking and straining at the leash, she may cautiously allow him to come into the rest of the house, though still on a leash. Eventually, when the dog proves calm and sound, the woman may extend a tentative hand towards the animal's head, etc, until it has been established that this dog is indeed different from the animal of her childhood experience.

This analogy may be applied when a child's only image of a father/protector has been one of an abuser. It is unlikely that the same child will leap at the opportunity to embrace a Heavenly Father, despite the reassurances of Christian friends. But if a person takes the reassurance of the Word of God that God most certainly is to be trusted as both protector and friend, a cautious relationship may ensue. With careful, small steps, the relationship will grow, as will the trust, until that person is fully assured of God's faithfulness.

The second story centres on sheep. Numerous times in the Bible, God's people are referred to as His sheep, and He as their Shepherd. In this story on trust, I am going to use sheep, the Australian sheep farm and farmer for an analogy.

On a farm, an ordinary lamb will be born out in the paddock, and will be cared for by its woolly mother. As a paddock lamb, it will learn that the farmer has scary motor bikes, barking, nipping dogs, noisy shearing machines, and 'oh, ouch!' sharp blades that painfully cut away its little backside, in a process the farmer calls mulesing. (I grew up on the farm amongst the sheep, and saw this nasty mulesing process many times. I was never impressed hearing the dear little lambs bleating so mournfully when they cut the flesh away). Still, back to the story. Even though the Aussie farmer will tell you that all of these devices and processes are for the health and well-being of the growing lamb, the lamb doesn't know this, and consequently learns all of the standard reactions expected of all sheep. It will learn to run away from the farmer, his dogs and any other curious onlookers. When it is being rounded up, it will always run the wrong way, and strangely, will even run headlong into any object, including fences, often repeatedly, in a wild, crazy panicked attempt to escape the worst of all horrors. It will not come when called. It will not go through the gate into the horrid little yards, where they stuff worm medicine down its throat. Basically, it has no mind to cooperate with the farmer and his intentions at all. Some insensitive farmers have been known to call such sheep-like behaviour stupid, and the sheep themselves "the dumbest blarmin' creatures you'd ever seen". These farmers have not understood the paddock lamb's state of emotional dysfunction. However, those farmers who know that God likens us to His sheep won't make such hasty comments.

There are other lambs that live on the farm. These are called pet lambs, and are brought in from the paddock perhaps a day or two after they are born. Usually they have been rescued from their dead mother, or some such other mishap. These little lambs are installed in front of the cheery kitchen fire, are fed warm milk by caring and concerned children, are cuddled and combed, and treated generally as another member of the family. These little lambs grow up knowing the farmer as the growling old fellow who totes the lamb away from the children to do all of those nasty little lamb jobs, and gives it back into the waiting arms of the distressed careers. The lamb is then over pampered until it has grown into an intelligent sheep, who knows just who is the boss, where its food comes from and will come the moment it is called. Invariably, the pet lamb will be exiled into the paddock, just as soon as it is old enough, and begins to create havoc in the family garden. It will never quite understand the other paddock sheep, and they don't ever quite mix together. And come shearing time, the pet lamb will bolt into the race, almost grinning, and nuzzle its owner with joy, looking for a sweet treat that it has become used to. The other sheep, confused, may follow its lead, but they have never lost their fear or mistrust.

Perhaps you can see two different sorts of people in this scenario. There are those pet lamb people, who have been brought up in the safety and security of a loving, God-fearing family; who have been taught to know and love their God and Maker. They are not afraid to trust Him, and they follow Him. They are not afraid to be open, for they know that God will comfort them in their hurt. Then there are the paddock lamb people who might know there is a God, just as the lamb knows there is a farmer, but their experience has not been one of security and a growing relationship. Rather, they have been bitten by the sheep dog, or infected by the blow-flies so many times that they doubt that God, or anyone else cares for them.

If we tried an experiment, taking an ordinary terrified sheep from the paddock, putting him in a small enclosure, and trying to get him to trust us as a human being, how long do you think it would take to win his trust? The answer, I imagine, would be a very, very long time.

Learning to trust and earning the right to be trusted both come over a long period of time.

What does trust mean to you

Does it mean: A	**or**	**Does it mean: B**
No fear		Constant doubt
Full confidence		Plain terror
Absolute assurance		Uncertainty
Knowing the risks are covered		Feeling naked vulnerability
Everything is under control		Everything is out of control

Full and complete trust in the Lord will only be perfected at our graduation into His presence at the end of our days. But it can be gradually increased, step-by-step, day-by-day, as we exercise faith and continually praise Him for answered prayers. But the closer we get to full trust in God, the more likely our feelings will reflect those of column A. We need to work at building our trust in God, as those feelings represented in column B are those of fear and terror, and very plainly would urge us toward being 'control freaks'.

Let us look at another analogy:
Picture trust as a hundred dollar note, then ask yourself the question, how much trust should I spend on any one individual. For example:

A balance caring parent	**$85.00**
Someone you have just met	**$2.50**
A reliable friend of many years	**$70.00**
A convicted criminal	**$2.50**
An implusive brother or sister	**$45.00**
An abusive guardian	**3 cents**
Our Heavenly Father	**$100.00**

Some people have gone foolishly through life, lavishly spending trust on anyone and everyone, not ever applying any wisdom to their emotional decisions, and when they get hurt by someone who has never earned their trust, and has a reputation of being untrustworthy, they harden their hearts and decide that they can no longer trust anyone at all. It is a swinging of the pendulum from foolish expenditure to no expenditure.

I have been caught in the trap myself, in the past, of being very open and trusting of anyone I met. I based my generous spirit upon the example of my father, who is a very open and trusting man. Both of us had been bought up in a small, closed country community, where everyone knew everyone, and generally speaking, everybody we knew in our small circle was a decent sort. This fostered in us the mistaken belief that the world at large was generally made up of decent people. Unfortunately, both my father and I discovered that there are people in the world who lie, and that some are unscrupulous, saying and promising one thing, with no intention of backing their word with honest action. It was a hard lesson to learn, and sad. Speaking for myself, and knowing my father as I do, neither of us really wants to believe that people are not what they pretend to be. I know that I would prefer to live in my own fairyland, believing that everybody I meet is honest, good at heart, and will always do the right thing by me. That's what I want to believe, but to actually stake the safety of my family on such a mistaken foundation would be nothing short of a disaster. I have to face the cold hard reality that some people do lie, and sometimes they don't even care that they lie.

Of course, I am on one end of the spectrum. The other end is where those who have suffered betrayal gather in their suspicious, hard circle, and refuse to trust even the smallest amount to anybody.
You see, where trusting another person is concerned, there are levels of trust. There are some people who over a lifetime have built an honest and stable reputation. These people have worked at the qualities of being reliable, integral, responsible etc and it is right to extend a good amount of trust to them. It is highly likely that your trust will be safe. Of course, it must be made clear that you should never trust any human being 100%.

You should never trust any human being 100%

There have been times in the past where I have thought that someone as respectable as a pastor, who occupies a high position of responsibility, should be implicitly trusted on all occasions, on every subject and at every turn. That is a nice thought, but not only will it yield disappointment for the truster soon enough, it is also tough for the trusted. Do you have any idea how hard it must be for someone in one of those high up positions, in the public eye, whose actions are open for scrutiny to the whole world? There have been one or two occasions where I have put some authority figure on a high pedestal; a place of display and honour, and a platform that is tiny, with no room to move; and when that person failed, as they were bound to sooner or later, they came crashing down from the pedestal. I didn't give them any room to fail, and that was not fair of me to put that expectation on another person. Human beings do fail, right from the Apostle Paul down to the convicted criminal just out on bail. The point is, some people fail less than others, and therefore can be trusted just a little more.

For those with a reliable reputation, it is fair to have a reasonably high expectation of what their performance will be, but when they do have a crisis, slip and fall, you should apply the grace of God, give them a little room, and forgive them as God in Heaven forgives you.
On the other hand, there are some whose reputation is one of constant unreliability. Depending on their area of failure, you should cut them a little slack - give them a go - and see if they use the opportunity to start rebuilding a new reputation.

When I say depending on the area of failure, I am going to qualify what I mean. If someone has had a problem with skimming the till, light-fingeredness, stealing, and you wish to give them the opportunity to turn over a new leaf, you need to ask yourself how much you can afford to lose in this exercise. You may be willing to risk $100, and give them a task that includes being responsible for that amount of money. If you do this, and you know the person's past reputation, you should be prepared to lose that amount of money. But give the person a go, and if they prove sound in that instance, you can credit that success over temptation to them, and next time they will have a little more credibility in your estimation. That credibility must be built up over a long period of time, and increased gradually.

Remember you should only risk what you can afford to lose.

But this is where it gets a little harder. If a person's area of failure has been in the harming of another person, particularly in the area of sexual assault, how can you ever trust them again? You can never afford to risk a child's life just to give them the opportunity to see if they can resist the temptation. This is a tough call, but just because a person repents, even if there are tears of remorse, doesn't mean that person has earned the right to be trusted with the lives of children again. I do not see that there is any way to regain trust once this area has been violated. A reformed alcoholic may walk past a pub and be overwhelmed by temptation, and have a fall. What has been lost? Some credibility, a few dollars, and a massive hangover. The damage has all been against self. But if a former paedophile claims he is recovered, and you foolishly trust him with the care of a child, and that person succumbs to the temptation again, you have lost a whole lot more than a bit of credibility. You have lost the innocence and emotional well being of a human being. That is a risk that no one can afford.

It is true, a person who has been trapped in the damaging lifestyle of harming other people may receive forgiveness, and may truly desire to be free of that devastating behaviour. He or she may wish to be integrated into a church family, and God gives that opportunity to every person who calls upon the name of the Lord and dies to self. But a wise church leadership will never install such a person in a job that has any influence over defenceless people. Such a person may get the job of helping set out the chairs, or helping fold the church newsletters, or perhaps even greeting people at the door.
But to give him or her a place where they may fall in temptation again is not only wrong against the potential victims, but also wrong for the person as well. If they were genuine in their desire to be free of that particular sin, they would never want to fall in it again. We must protect both parties from such a disaster.

You can increase trust - both trusting someone and being trusted.

If you wish to help someone improve his or her reputation, or you wish to improve your own, there is some work to be done, and it will take time.

Firstly, regard a person as a bank account. At one stage the amount of trust in that person's account may be '0', or even worse may be in deep debt.

If you extend them a little trust, and they return it faithfully to you, then you can credit it to their account. Try again, a little bit more next time, and if they return it to you once again, another credit. A person may make a deposit or withdrawal in your estimation, depending on their behaviour.

The amount of trust you invest in a person really depends on the amount they have deposited.

You should not really trust a stranger with a whole amount, on first acquaintance, unless that stranger comes with high recommendations from someone else whose opinion you trust.

When learning to trust God for the very first time, try investing a little bit at a time, and you will find that He is faithful. There will come a time when, like Paul in *2 Timothy 1:12b*, you will be *convinced* that He will guard that which you have entrusted to Him.

There is just one more thing that you should note. There are times when we may have been foolish - times when we've made up our minds how it is that God should act on our behalf. Even though we may have zealously proclaimed that God is going to do this or do that, and may actually be believing for something positive, it is true that most of us, at one time or another, have presumed that we know what God has in mind. If you have ever done this, you need to be reassured that there are many people who have fallen into this trap, myself included. We've made the loud and arrogant announcements on God's behalf, and then "trust" or rather expect that God will now need to patch up, or make up or fix up a situation that He never meant us to be in in the first place.

God will never let us down, in that He knows what is the very best for us. We must not blame Him, then, if he allows us to handle the "consequences" of our own impulsive, disobedient action.

Read *Proverbs 19:20-21; Proverbs 12:15; Proverbs 13:10; Psalm 33:11*

chapter seven

AN EXTRA CHAPTER ON TRUST

It's a really big subject

When studying the dictionary definitions of the word 'trust', depending on whether it is a verb or a noun, it has two different applications.

In the previous chapter we have been looking at 'trust' as a noun when in reference to a confidence, a foundation to rely on etc, in basic reference to our 'trust in God'. We also looked at 'trust' as a verb, the act of placing confidence in someone, in basic reference to our trusting other people.

God created us with the ability to both trust and to be trusted, but with the fall of man at the time of Adam and Even, came sin and betrayal, and every human being since has struggled with this issue.

Many of life's experiences have shaped our inner responses, and many people find it difficult to be vulnerable (as discussed previously). So to trust God seems difficult, sometimes impossible. To trust others is sometimes equally difficult. But ultimately, an individual will trust something, even if it comes down to trusting themselves, and hence the beginning of an independent, rebellious lifestyle.

Read 2 *Chronicles 20:20; Psalm 4:5 &8; Psalm 118:5-9; Proverbs 11:28; Isaiah 26:3-4; Psalm 146:3-7; 2 Chronicles 32:7-8; Isaiah 31:1-3; Psalm 37:3-7*

In a world where one of the most common adages to live by is: 'What's in it for me?' we find a generation of people who plea-bargain with God.

So long as they get all the promises and benefits, they will consider trusting in God.

But the minute something happens that they don't like, or that makes them unhappy or uncomfortable, then blaming God seems like an easy solution. Facing tests and trials was not in the original contract. Whatever happened to the blessings?

The three young men whose story is told in *Daniel 3:15-18* were wonderful examples of what real trust is all about. Their names were Shadrach, Meshach and Abednego, and they were young Hebrew boys who had been taken captive from their native land when the Babylonians overran Israel. At the point where this story takes place, the Babylonian king, Nebuchadnezzar, had made a decree that everyone in the land was to bow down and worship a golden statue of himself that had been set up. But these three young men refused to go against the law of God, and even though disobedience meant that they would be thrown bound, and alive, into a fiery furnace, they refused to bow to the statue.

They were not tempted by Nebuchadnezzar's threats, and boldly confessed their unwavering trust in the Lord, declaring that their God, whom they served, was well able to deliver them from the blazing fire. Then came the real test of their faith, when they said, 'But if He does not deliver us, we still will not serve your gods or worship the golden image'.
This example of unshakeable faith has been repeated over and over again as evidenced by the lives of the thousands of Christian martyrs who have valiantly faced torture and death, literally unable to deny their faith in God. It must be noted that martyrs are not just a group of people from history, men and women who were thrown to the lions during Roman times.

It is reported that there are literally thousands of martyrs that die every week in certain parts of the world, showing their persecutors that their faith in God cannot be shaken even in the face of physical death.

THIS IS GREAT FAITH AND TRUST IN GOD.

The Scripture does everything from suggesting, commanding, requiring, begging to pleading with us to trust in the Lord our God; and yet living as human beings in a fallen world, there are several things that seem to inhibit this.

1. PRIDE/SELF SUFFICIENCY

Read *Jeremiah 17: 5-10; Daniel 4:28-37*
How many times are we, as very 'human' beings, tempted to puff our chests out with pride and mentally pat ourselves on the back, thinking how clever we are, and what a good job we do, etc. And further to this, we indulge in the feeling that if we are not involved in the project, it probably won't work. Now, to put things into perspective, it is true that God uses our very 'human' bodies and minds to accomplish His purposes. This works especially well when

we are obedient to Him. So God sort of does need us, in a sense, but he certainly doesn't need our pride and independence. That He could probably do without. He does let us go on our merry way at times, but we need to be mindful of pride and where it took Nebuchadnezzar in the story in Daniel.
Read *Daniel 4:28-37* Nebuchadnezzar was the King of Babylon, and was very powerful, having conquered the known world of that time. He had built a lot of stuff too, and in this story we see him wandering on the rooftop of his palace, surveying the land and all that he had conquered and all that he'd built. In his heart he began to boast over what a marvellous job he'd done, and how great he was, and that it had all been because of him. He became full of pride, and believed that it was his own skill and talent that had brought him to all this. Even before the words had come out of his mouth, God struck him with a curse of insanity, and he became crazed, thinking he was an animal, and for several years he lived in the fields, totally mad. Then God allowed his reason to return, and Nebuchadnezzar not only realised his stupid pride, but also confessed it out loud, finally admitting that God is the giver of all power and authority.

We need to keep this story of Nebuchadnezzar's pride in mind. Confidence is good, and skill is good, but if we are particularly gifted with confidence and skill, we need to be extra mindful of our own susceptibility to pride and self-sufficiency. Read *Psalm 8:3-4; Jeremiah 18:3-6; Isaiah 55:7-11; Psalm 103:13-17*

We are like grasshoppers in His sight, and the grass that withers. Our glory, if at all, is temporary and passes like the seasons. The only thing that will ever last for us is the effort we invest in building God's kingdom, and this only if we build in obedience to His Word. We can build plenty, and be thinking it is all for the Lord, but only that which He has called us to build will last. *Psalm 127:1* tells us that unless the Lord is building the house, those of us that are working are wasting our time.
Resist the temptation to lapse into the thinking that 'I can do it on my own' or 'I did it my way'. The sooner we come to the realisation that all the successes we have by God's grace and mercy working out in our lives, the better off we'll be. Without Him, we are nothing.

2. BETRAYAL/FEAR

This is another thing that greatly hinders us in our endeavours to trust God. I went into this in some detail in the previous chapter, and it may be good to review it at this point.

It is doubtful that any single one of us has totally mastered the ability to completely trust God, free from any fear or doubt.

Still, we need to press toward that goal and face the fears squarely.

3. IGNORANCE

It is quite natural, thanks to our fallen nature, to be independent, fearful, untrusting, anxious, rebellious etc. We don't need anybody to teach us these things; they will grow in our lives all on their own, rather like weeds in a garden. They don't need to be watered or encouraged to grow. They flourish easily. If there is no other input, say for example, Sunday School, godly parent or grandparent etc, to discourage fear and rebellion, and to encourage steps towards growth in faith and trust, it is unlikely that a child will hear about it on television or in the school yard.
Hence, our third stumbling block toward trust - Ignorance.

We live in a world that encourages foolish ideas - 'You are your own man'; 'Watch out for number one'; 'Don't let anyone push you around'; 'Stand up for your rights'; 'You don't need anyone else'; 'God is for the weak-minded'; 'Watch out you don't get involved with a cult where they do the thinking for you'.
Such ideas as these are not just popular, but almost an accepted part of our society's thinking. It is frustrating to realise that because of manipulative, abusive and controlling authority that has been found at times in both the world and the church, some of these points have taken on some validity.

And yet, it all flies in the face of trusting God. While we are busily teaching people to set boundaries, we must be careful to balance that teaching with encouragement to allow their faith and trust to grow.

Sadly, there are too many adults who are hearing for the first time about the need to trust in God.

By the time a person is an adult, they will already be firmly entrenched in behavioural patterns that reflect independence, suspicion, fear, rebellion etc. There have been times when I have tried to teach a new convert the whole of 'life's principles God's way' in two lessons, and usually it is a dismal failure.

If a person has never heard about trust in God before, it is unlikely that they have practised it. As a Christian worker, I have to accept the fact that it is going to take time for new converts to grab a hold of the principle, and to become adept at using it. After all, even for those of us who have been taught the Word right from the start, we still had to struggle with our own brand of doubt and independence.

4. REBELLION

We can either be rebellious but ignorant of the fact, or we can be rebellious and know full well what we're up to.

The following is just a short list of words that are synonymous with 'rebellion': Disobedient, undisciplined, naughty, difficult, self-willed, wayward, unruly, unmanageable, unwilling, insubordinate, mutinous, contrary, opposing, uncompliant, resisting, challenging, obstinate, revolutionary, reactionary, seditious, traitorous, treasonous, untamed. In short - **NOT NICE!**

Read *Psalm 107:8-15; Isaiah 63:7-11; 1Samuel 15:22-26; 1Samuel 12:14-16; Ezekiel 20:18-26; Psalm 78:5-8; Jeremiah 5:21-25*

God's people, the Israelites, were constantly disobeying God, over and over again. Independence, fear, lust, greed and temptation seemed to be so alluring that they easily gave way to sin, and when they did, they did it in a big way. Over and over, God sent prophets to warn, beg, plead and eventually threaten them to turn from disobedience and rebellion, but often it wasn't until calamity had fully settled on them that they would turn their hard hearts back to the Lord their God.

Today, as Christians, we can easily picture a rebel as some young bikie-looking person, with fifteen earrings inserted in the oddest of places, black leather clothes, a shaved head with just one piece of hair left long. It is easy enough to brand this stereotype with the name rebel, but in fact we have all taken our turn at being rebellious. Just from the list above, there are words that jump off the page that could easily be applied to attitudes that we have indulged in at one time or another. And while we have been busy resisting authority, questioning counsel and ignoring directives, we have in fact had our attention diverted from the very Person in our lives who requires ultimate obedience and trust. The Lord, our God and Father.

Disobedience does not necessarily have to take an extreme outward appearance. We can be resisting, undermining and stubborn on the inside and still look like Joe or Suzie Christian on the outside.

The trouble is, when we practise this type of rebellion, it also undermines our faith and trust in God. Rebellion is like a weed, which seems to just pop up out of nowhere, because we can't see the creeping root system. Our full trust and faith in God can never come when we do not obey His Word.

Discussing further the concept of trusting in man:

Without negating the Scriptures that tell us we should not put our trust in man, we must learn to trust mankind. Our trust (noun -object) must be in God. The thing we build our lives on, the thing we hold as a foundation for our lives - our trust - must be in God.
But there are plenty of times that we must trust in man. This is a more temporary, passing action. The verb to trust means acceptance that what a person says is true, and that they will not bring harm to you.
A child is born with no real option other than to trust its parents. Its very existence depends on the parents' willingness to care for and nurture him or her. This is the way God has designed it to be.

Parents are supposed to be a role model for who God the Father is.

Obviously, not every parent represents God's lovingkindness and goodness. In fact, all too often they exhibit the very opposite.

But just suppose that the parents are responsible, loving, caring and attentive. In these cases, the children will probably grow up trusting their parents, and, depending on the parents' attitude towards others, trusting other people as well. We try to teach our children that law-enforcement officers are to be trusted; that teachers are to be trusted; that ministers are to be trusted, etc. It is easy enough to find examples of where corruption and depravity has bred and been practised under the cloak of respectability of these positions, and it is cause for some nervousness when we have to consider trusting other people.
But the only other option is to teach children fear and suspicion. Here is where we must carefully balance the scales. Teach 'stranger danger' and the like, but we must be careful not to teach them rebellion towards authority (i.e. to challenge, resist and undermine).

Children need to be taught to thoughtfully trust, and they need to be taught to be trustworthy (responsible).

Families, churches, governments and societies need elements of trust between individuals in order to function.

A good reputation is built through consistent acts of responsibility.

In other words, a person builds a reputation that they can be trusted (relied upon). Other people know that they can trust this person, and that they will not be let down, because trustworthiness has been demonstrated over and over again.

The converse is also true. A person can have a bad reputation because they have proved themselves to be unreliable, irresponsible and a liability to have around. This happens all too often. Sometimes a person might be new in the church community, having come from a background of consistent acts of criminal behaviour. This person will not have a great chance of being trusted - not for a long time. Depending on the degree of sin (that is to say that all sin is deserving of death in God's eyes, but not all sin has the same effects of devastation on other people) as to how quickly or slowly their trustworthiness becomes established.

Great wisdom must be applied when helping a person establish credibility. If their negative habit has been one of substance abuse, then a fall will hurt only themselves, but if it has involved the abuse of other people, a fall will result in devastating effects on other people's lives. Sometimes the possible consequences are not worth the risk involved, as I have stated in the previous chapter.

As growing Christians, we should become more and more willing to risk a part of ourselves in an effort to help other people gain confidence in being trusted. It's not always easy, but someone has to turn the other cheek, go the extra mile, and give up his or her coat. Read *Matthew 5:39-42*

Also Christian growth involves the producing of fruit, including the fruits of patience, long-suffering, endurance, not holding an account of wrongs done, etc. In an effort to grow, new Christians are inevitably going to fail. We must be willing to give them time to get it right. (This is not necessarily an excuse for them to carelessly and thoughtlessly take advantage of a softy).

chapter eight

DEVELOPING DISCERNMENT

Whom do I trust and when?

At the end of chapter six, I made some reference to those times when we may have made a huge decision, planned the outcome, and staked it all on trusting God's intervention. Sometimes those situations work out miraculously and sometimes they don't. What is the key element to it? Does God sometimes lead us to a dead end, like He did with the children of Israel when they were fleeing from Egypt, with the purpose of extending our faith? Is it that sometimes we have waltzed out on a branch with great zeal and passion, based more on our own assumptions than on what God has said? And there is the question of how you tell the difference?

I cannot sit here and say that I have the one hundred percent, fool-proof formula for you to use, because if I did, then I would either be a very rich person, or I would be God, and I'm neither.

But I can discuss discernment, and write some points that you can use to help you tell the difference in situations.

First of all, to define 'discern': *to see or understand the difference; to make a distinction, as in to discern between right and wrong, truth and lie.*

Read *1 Kings 3:9-12; Hebrews 5:11-14; Deuteronomy 32:28-29; Proverbs 8:1-17; Proverbs 16:21*

To trust; or not to trust. Better yet, when to trust or whom should I trust.

There are varying levels of trust, and wisdom and discernment are the tools that help us decide whom, when and how much. Every person in this life needs to develop trustworthiness - that doesn't necessarily mean that every person will apply the diligence needed and earn that reputation.Still, as Christians, love and compassion begs us to give people a second chance; third chance; twenty-fourth chance. But love and compassion should not be an excuse for foolishness - a careless casting of pearls before swine. We really do need to develop some discernment.

1. LEARNING DISCERNMENT THROUGH THE WORD OF GOD

The Scripture in *Hebrews 5:11-14* talks of the more mature Christian who has come past eating only milk, and has progressed onto the solid word of God, and says that solid food is for the mature, because through practice they have trained their senses to discern good and evil. In other words, the mature have done the elementary lessons, and have moved on to the solid Word of God. How important it is to not only be hearers of God's Word, but doers also, actively practising what we have learned to be truth.

My mother-in-law makes authentic lasagne. She does not buy one manufactured product to use. She makes the pasta herself from flour and eggs, she makes the sauce herself from tomato and basil and garlic that she has grown in the garden. She selects the steak she wants to use and has the butcher mince only the finest pieces. She uses free-range eggs, and buys the real sheep-milk (parmesan) cheese and grates it herself. The final product tastes like nothing else. I have not ever been to an Italian restaurant and tasted anything as authentic.
But before I had tasted the real thing, I was under the impression that lasagne was made by boiling those hard packet noodle sheets, frying up a bit of mince, add a jar of Dolmio spaghetti sauce, bung in a bit of cheese sauce, and there it was. It tasted all right, and was easy enough to make. The point is, it was a poor imitation of the real thing, but I didn't know that until I had tasted the real thing. And then there was the job of discerning the difference between the restaurant lasagne and Nonna's authentic recipe. Only after many times of trying the real thing did I learn what the authentic stuff was really supposed to taste like.

The Scripture in Hebrews is telling us that we need to know what God's Word and truth tastes like. We need to partake of it often so that we can then tell the difference between it and the counterfeit.

2. LEARNING DISCERNMENT THROUGH WISE COUNSEL

Read *Proverbs 2:1-5; Proverbs 1:2-5; Proverbs 13:10; Proverbs 15:22, 15:31-32*
Here is a fine example of what it means to trust man. God has given to us authority figures, and in the majority of instances they are men and women of integrity, maturity and discernment. This does not necessarily mean that they are perfect and beyond making a mistake.

When we go for counsel, whether it is to our parents, spouse, teachers or pastors, wisdom tells us to measure up the counsel against the Word of God. On the one hand, counsel should confirm what God is speaking to our hearts. On occasion counsel will bring a check or caution at times when we are moving too fast and not discerning properly. These are often times when we become emotionally involved in situations and we cannot see things objectively (i.e. from an outsider's point of view).

In the world, there is a class of people who have refined the art of lying. They have successfully lied to themselves, and are almost convinced that they are right, and it is just a simple step from there to presenting a false image to other people. Whether the lying is deliberate or not, there is a spirit of deception that is at work; a deception that says, "what I want to be true, must be true. My version of reality is the only one, everyone else is wrong." As maturing Christians we must keep our hearts open to discern the times when we are being 'had'.
As I stated before, when we become emotionally involved with people - in a friendship or even in a helping capacity - we often cannot see the deceptions that are being played on us. Sometimes, much to our annoyance, a trusted friend or counsellor may point out the very thing we cannot see. Sometimes we don't want to see it. But wisdom begs us to listen to our counsellors. The more we practise this, the sharper we will become in seeing the truth for ourselves.

3. LEARNING DISCERNMENT THROUGH THE VOICE OF THE SPIRIT

Read *John 14:16-17; John 14:26; 1John 5:7-8*

Jesus was very reassuring when He promised that he would send the helper - the Holy Spirit - whose very job it is to guide us into all truth, to teach and to comfort. But we need to tune our spiritual ear to the voice of the Spirit. We need to spend time before Him, away from the many other distractions that want to drown out the voice of the Spirit. This is particularly important when one is starting out on a new relationship venture, whether it be work, friendship or counselling. We must allow the voice of the Holy Spirit to impress upon us either His peace or His caution. Read *1Corinthians 12:4-11; 1Corinthians 14:1*
God has made available the gifts of word of wisdom, word of knowledge and distinguishing of spirits. We must earnestly desire these sorts of gifts and practise using them. When discerning a person's spirit, one gets a general

impression from body language, the look that is in a person's eyes (the eye is the window of the soul), and sometimes there is a feeling that one cannot define. We cannot sign a contract on just these feelings, but if you do feel a 'check' in your spirit, it is probably wisdom to proceed only with caution. Check with the other sources - i.e. Word of God, counsel etc.

4. LEARNING DISCERNMENT THROUGH AUTHORITY

When we are merrily going along on a project, happy with how things are progressing, it is a 'spanner in the works' to have an authority figure question the procedure. And yet, God has placed authority figures in our lives, as has been said over and over again. The thing about listening and submitting to authority is that the person in authority is the one who then assumes the responsibility for the success or failure of the project. Even if we don't agree, we are free to express our doubt, but ultimately, if we submit, we may find ourselves protected from making a huge error of judgement.

If, on the other hand, we turn out to be right, it isn't our responsibility anymore. Because someone is in authority does not automatically mean that they are all-knowing and immune to making mistakes. It does mean though, that they are responsible for looking out for those under their care, and if they have a 'check' in their spirit, then they are responsible for looking into it.

And one last little bit of advice on trust:
Don't borrow trouble; take one crisis at a time!

chapter nine

LOOKING PAST NUMBER ONE

Learning to relate to other people

"Me, myself, I -Me, myself, I"

There is actually a song that has those three words, and that sentiment, as its theme. The great god of the western world is the god of self, and we have our altars of worship and sacrifice - our bathroom mirrors for a start.
When in the third world, people have stone idols, occult practices and fundamentalist religious persecutions to stifle and discourage their Christian faith, we of the western world have ourselves, and sometimes, I'm almost convinced that fighting the allurements of the god of self might be harder to defeat than what comes against our third world brothers and sisters.
Now you might say that is perfectly ridiculous - that facing physical and mental torture and persecution has to be one hundred times harder on a person than trying to battle selfishness. To be sure, I'm not one to want to swap, and submit myself to the horrors that some of these Christian martyrs have to face. I'm not really into physical discomfort. But I have also begun to realise that there is a strange sort of monster within all of us. We perhaps don't recognise it, but the Bible calls it our flesh or old self. Read *Romans 8:3-17; Romans 13:14; Ephesians 2:1-7; Galatians 5:13-26*. It's very important that you read these Scriptures.

Even for someone like myself, who has been brought up in the church, and has practised Christianity for as long as I can remember, who is well versed in the Bible and has not had a great deal of experience practising the worldly vices, I still recognise the flesh in me. There are times that the temptations of self and the flesh are strong, as with every man or woman, and times when we all fall prey to it. Perhaps I will never be tempted to go out and rob a bank, or never be tempted to murder someone. There is little point in those sorts of temptations for me, as I simply am not weak in those areas. But there are areas where I am weak - and those usually come under the banner of self.

Pride, jealousy, laziness, selfishness come to my mind often, and the society and culture in which I live make it very very easy for me to succumb to their charms.

In it all, I have noticed this principle: At those times when I have been fervent in prayer and seeking God's presence, reading His Word and praising Him, I find the flesh 'monster' is not very strong, and its temptations don't really have much kick to them. However, if I have been feeding the self 'monster' with all sorts of self-indulgences, any practice that may not necessarily be wrong in itself, but is distracting me away from God and the heart of God, then the self 'monster' seems quite strong, and my spirit is somewhat weak in its ability to resist the temptations.

Now, when we come to take stock of the way we relate to other people - whether it be close family, intimate friend or work place associate - we need to polish up our honesty microscope again. There are all sorts of different relating styles, some of them yielding easily in a get-along-well sort of relationship, and some producing arguments, differences, fire and spitting at every turn.

The Bible makes it fairly clear that our old flesh is self-seeking, and if we go along our merry way, making our basic standard of reference the way we feel, I can fairly well predict the outcome of certain relationships.

Read *Romans 2:8*

The fact of the matter is: Every one of us likes it how we like it!

That might not seem like much of a revelation to you, but if you think about it a bit more, and analyse your own motives, you will begin to see what I eventually saw.

I have always liked myself as a person, and have lived under the general impression that everybody else liked me too. It came as somewhat of a shock when I first realised that not everybody in the world liked me, (I was about 23 at the time). I was dumbfounded, flabbergasted, stunned and amazed. You see, I saw the world and the people in it purely from my own perspective. I liked people, and as I said in earlier chapters, I wanted to believe that everybody was trustworthy and good. As far as I was concerned, my motives were pure, and I had no mind or heart to hurt anybody.

But that didn't mean that I didn't hurt anybody. I did, apparently, and that came simply because I made decisions and acted according to my own selfish wants and desires. I summed situations up according to how I thought things were, and worked towards outcomes that I thought would be good for me.

In all of this, my motivation was pure enough, but my perspective was very narrow and self-centred.

From my observation of the world, I've come to the conclusion that I'm not much different from most other people.

There is a scarce breed of people who have really understood the life and example of Christ, and have actively followed after it, sacrificing their own wants for others. A woman like Mother Theresa is a classic example. And there are many others as well. That does not mean that those people are any better than you or me, or more deserving of Christ's love and forgiveness. They will have made mistakes the same as us all. But folks like that have really taken hold of their 'flesh' and brought it into submission to the Spirit of God, and have followed His call - and have changed the world in the process.

We all have the opportunity to do the same, even if the world we change is the little bit of territory that immediately surrounds us.

Read *Galatians 5:16-26 and Romans 7:15-25 and 8:1-11*

Paul outlines clearly the constant battle that rages within all of us between our flesh and the new life Spirit of God that now dwells in us.

In *Romans 7,* Paul tells us of his own struggle with that inner monster, and how he often found himself failing, but later, in Chapter 8 he is more confident in his recommendation of making sure we 'walk in the Spirit'. He emphasises this principle in great detail in *Galatians 5,* and even outlines for us the results that will come if we follow the pull of the flesh. The list, as taken from the Living Bible translation, includes: impure thoughts, eagerness for lustful pleasure (immorality), idolatry (putting anything higher than God, and living our lives for it), spiritism (sorcery or encouraging the activity of demons), hatred and fighting, jealousy and anger, constant effort to get the best for yourself, complaints and criticisms, the feeling that only those of your association are right and that everyone else is wrong, envy, murder, drunkenness and wild sorts of parties.

Now let us use our logic for a moment. If these sorts of things are the results of our allowing the flesh to dominate our lives, it follows that we are going to be having a lot of relationship conflict. There are not many people that I know who actually enjoy being around a person who is bitter, jealous, angry, alcoholic, sexually unfaithful, critical, complaining, selfish. There are a lot of people trapped in domestic situations who live with these sorts of attributes in their spouse, but it is not enjoyable, and certainly could not be called love.

Perhaps you might not feel that you have all of those dreadful symptoms in your life, maybe only one or two, but still, the conclusion is that it is there as a result of our feeding the flesh and starving the Spirit. Not only that, but any one of those above complaints, if given enough time to work, can effectively destroy any relationship all on its own.

But Paul doesn't leave it there in *Galatians 5.* He then goes on to tell of the fruit that grows in the life of a person who yields constantly to the Spirit. That list includes: Love, joy, peace, patience, kindness, goodness, faithfulness, gentleness, and self-control. Paul's basic summary is that there isn't any law against these types of attitudes.

But don't just skim over that list without proper thought. Take time to look at each attribute and understand what it really means. Just take 'love' as an example.

'Love', the word that has been so misunderstood and incorrectly defined.

The worldly idea of love is something that is sex-related; it is sweaty palms, and thundering heart rate; it is dizzy mind, unable to think of anything but the person you're in 'love' with. It is being together all the time. It is sex. When you boil that definition down to its basic core, all you will find is that 'love' is self-gratification.

But the Bible has a very different definition of 'love'.

Read *1 Corinthians 13:4-8*

Here is a definition that is totally self-less. Such words as patience and kindness immediately feature. Then there are a whole bunch of things that love is not: it is not jealous, not arrogant, does not brag, is not haughty or selfish or rude, it does not seek its own way, it is not easily provoked, and doesn't take into account every little wrong suffered. It is never glad about unrighteousness, in fact it mourns over injustice, but in turn it rejoices over truth and righteousness. It bears all things, believes all things, hopes all things, and endures all things. Love never fails.

Can you imagine being in a normal type of family relationship and making daily decisions based on the fruits of the Spirit and on the attributes of love? You see, at the moment, most of us make decisions, and then act according to how we feel.

Generally speaking, three different areas influence our emotions: Our preferences; our moods, and our perceptions.

Our **preferences** are shaped firstly by the type of personality that we are. For instance, I am a creative sort of personality and would prefer to read a book or practise the piano than go out shopping. I'm not sure what sort of personality likes shopping, but my husband has one of those and I don't. When it comes to preferences, there is great potential for an argument in our household, especially if either one of us insists upon our particular preference. Also culture has great influence on our preference. As you may have guessed from my sheep stories, I was brought up in an Australian rural culture and this is in stark contrast to my husband's urban Italian culture. When it comes to preference, I like the wide-open dusty plains, looking out across the paddocks of sheep; he likes the busy cosmopolitan café lifestyle. Such differing preferences leave great opportunity for argument, if either one of us refuses to apply the attributes of love and selflessness.

Our **moods** are also responsible for the way our emotions feel at a particular time. A person's mood can be affected by a number of variables. Firstly there is the effect that hormones play on a woman's moods. You only have to be a woman to know what I'm talking about here. I don't need to go into that! Secondly, a person's state of health can affect their mood.

Ill health or physical handicap can greatly influence how a person is feeling.

Discouragement, despair and frustration all build easily if a person is constantly battling ill health, and these in turn reduce a person's tolerance and ability to look positively upon a situation.

Thirdly, amounts of sleep can affect a person's mood. If a person is receiving the full quota of sleep that individual requires (I'm a 9 hour person myself, while my brother-in-law seems to need no more than 4 or 5 hours) mood will generally be influenced positively.

However, if a person is experiencing broken sleep, or greatly reduced sleep, it is obvious that their mood is not going to be particularly positive. If somebody prevents me from getting the required amount of sleep, my family knows that somebody will pay the next day - it isn't pleasant!

Fourthly, stress levels can and do affect mood. People who work under high levels of expectation and responsibility, and come home to similar levels of stress will find their mood will be affected.

Fifthly I had written down that the moon affects mood, but I don't have any concrete evidence. It's good to have a fifth point though!

The third thing that often affects our emotions is one's perceptions. A person's perceptions are very much influenced by previous experience. In the following illustration I have shown what I refer to as the 'experience filter'. In this illustration, the childhood experience of rejection has built in an automatic filter toward adult experience. As an adult, our character may come across a small instance of rejection, but because of the childhood experience, his perception is filtered and his emotions register it as far greater than it actually is. An experience filter could be positive or negative. The point is, our perception is affected by past experience.

Also, our perceptions are influenced by our learning environment. My perception of the weather is very much influenced by my learning environment of my father constantly watching the skies, talking about the rain, measuring the rain, and rejoicing about the rain. When it rains now, I usually rejoice, and go outside to measure it. I see rain as a positive thing. And yet, my husband sees the rain as a miserable nuisance. His perception of rain is like that of most urban dwellers. They can't go to the beach, and they can't hang out the clothes. A different learning environment yields a different perception.

Having seen just how much there is that affects the way we feel, we can see that there will be all kinds of different emotions, and if we act according to them, there will be many different types of actions.

This is where relationships come to grief. If we are in a close relationship like marriage, or even that of a parent/child relationship, we cannot simply act according to our own moods, preferences and perceptions. Well, we can, but conflict will be the inevitable outcome. Conflict, I have noted, is not generally healthy in any relationship. If pleasing ourself is the basis from which we work, then I can only see disaster for relationships. However, if we choose to adopt a new basis to work from, that of denying self and loving others, as the Bible defines love, then we are in a whole new ball game.

As I intimated before, denying self is not a popular pastime in this culture. It is not practised much, nor is it particularly encouraged. To choose to live like this will take some serious listening to the Spirit of God. Remember our old 'flesh' self will not like this sort of decision very much, and will most likely throw a colourful tantrum.

If you can see that this sort of decision-making basis will be helpful for the way you treat other people, then I strongly encourage you to read the following Scriptures to further boost your courage in this decision.

Read
Matthew 5:1-14&21,38,43; Matthew 22:35-40; Philippians 2:3;
Matthew 20:25; Matthew 7:1-6; 2Corinthians 1:12; Hebrews 13:16.
All of Hebrews 13; Hebrews 3:6;
Proverbs 15:1; Proverbs 28:1; Galatians 6:1-4.

Once you have read all of these Scriptures, we can compile a list of attributes that are healthy for us to use in relating to other people:

Relating with

Openness
Submission to one another
Love
Preferring others before yourself
Confidence in God's work in us
Kindness
Gentleness
Self-control
Servant attitude
Humility
Firm, but loving action
Conviction of truth

Problems that will inhibit good relations:

Arrogance
Pride
Hypocrisy
Manipulative control
Selfishness
Impatience
Inverted pride (painful introversion)
Criticism (picking/carping)
Stupidity or neutral thinking (blindly accepting other's intentions)

Before entering into a full scale war with your friend, child or spouse, ask yourself lots of questions, the most important being: what is the Biblical response to this thing that I'm feeling? Is it flesh or is it Spirit. The choice is always yours!

chapter ten

UNDERSTANDING ACCEPTANCE AND WORTH

Understanding our acceptance and worth basically comes down to understanding ourselves; not as a product of bad modelling, bad parenting or bad experience (our old self), but as a product of salvation, born into new life, no longer shackled by sin and unrighteousness, free from guilt and shame. Most importantly, we must know and understand that we have been bought with a price, the precious life and blood of Jesus Christ, and as a result of our faith in Him and obedience to His Spirit's leading, we become a child of God.
Read *Romans 8:14-17*
We have talked much about resisting the pull of our old 'flesh' self and walking instead in the way of the Holy Spirit. At this point I would like us to consider just what salvation really means. In days gone by, the word 'conversion' used to be applied to people who gave their hearts to the Lord, and became saved. In the recent era, the word 'converted' has been bandied about in a somewhat derogatory fashion, almost mocking the process. Even the phrase 'born-again' is being used in a joking type of way, and yet if those who spoke lightly of this wonderful transformation really understood what it meant, they would be taking hold of it for themselves, not joking about it.
Read *Galatians 2:20; Romans 6:4-12; Ephesians 4:22-24;2 Corinthians 5:15-17:* These Scriptures are very important to read and understand.

Of late I have wondered about the whole concept of salvation, or being converted. There are people that I know, who formerly lived terrible lives, full of all sorts of obvious and destructive sin, who, when they were saved or converted, became totally different people. Something happened in them that penetrated right to the very depths of their being and they could not go back to the person they were even if they had wanted to. On the other hand, and perhaps more commonly, I have known people who have been 'saved' more as a result of a Christian friend almost begging or bribing them to make that decision. The attitude of that person was still weighted heavily with self-pity, self-indulgence and self-centredness. Perhaps they agreed to attend church and other growth courses, but nothing seemed to change in them. There was no wonderful revelation of the love of God, the power of God, the righteousness of God or of any change that God could do on their behalf. These Christians always struggled, constantly pulled down by the things of the world, and the emotional threats were often offered; that if God wouldn't help them in the place they were, they would simply give up on God.

Now, as time has passed, there have been many, many excuses offered as to why some people don't break through, and as to why they continually threaten to drop out of Christianity. I may have even discussed some of these reasons in earlier chapters. But when it all boils down, the core fact remains:

***A person must know they are saved,
and must know that there is no other option
than to know, love, follow and obey their
Lord and Saviour, Jesus Christ.***

Our current 'take-no-responsibility' culture seems to be bending over backward molly-coddling some individuals, making excuses, and continually taxing the aid organizations with heavy burdens of counselling and charity.

Now God has called each of us to bear one another's burdens, to feed the hungry and poor, and to visit the prisoners and lonely. But that is not what I'm talking about. I'm really talking about an attitude that we unwittingly feed that keeps people bound in their own self-centred existence. The Word of God is quite clear that we are new creatures in Christ, that old things have passed away, and that all things are made new.

Now I know that there are some emotional issues that need to be worked through, and that this process takes time. I also know that a person's mind needs to be constantly renewed, especially if it has been in darkness for over twenty years. But the fact is, the moment we confess Jesus Christ as our Lord and Saviour, and believe that in our heart, we become a new creation, and a child of God. We have got to get this truth into our mind and into our heart as a revelation.

It must become the foundation upon which we build the rest of our 'saved' life. Even when we face trials and temptations; periods of despair and discouragement, nothing can ever change this foundation.

It is there for all eternity, and we must have it firmly fixed in our thinking. Circumstances, feelings and the lying voice of the devil will all try to remind us of the past, and will often rise up to cloud the truth. It is in this spiritual and emotional fog that we need to look to the compass of truth. The knowledge of what we have become in Christ.

You may recall the story "The Prince and the Pauper" by Mark Twain. The story goes that a poor young boy, the son of a cruel, abusive father, wandered by the palace gates one day, and as he watched he was met by another boy about his own age. It was the prince of the land who had longed to know what lay beyond the walls of his gilded cage. The prince proposed an exchange with the pauper, that while he went out to investigate the world outside the palace gates, the poor lad would don the prince's rich clothes, and sit in his apartments, so that he would not be missed. In Mark Twain's story, the boys were actually remarkably alike, and so after some time, when the prince had experienced enough and wanted to return to the palace, the guards would not believe he was anything other than a presumptuous pauper. Meanwhile, the other lad was confused and bewildered as the rest of the palace staff treated him as if he were the prince. Neither boy was able to convince anybody that they were not whom they appeared to be.

Now during the whole story of the prince's adventures in the dangerous outside world, he never ever believed he was anything other than the prince. Even when the pauper's horrible father caught hold of him and beat him mercilessly for telling such 'lies', the prince still maintained that he was the prince, and that he should not be treated in this way. That didn't mean that his circumstances miraculously changed, or that he was treated royally. In fact the opposite; as he was beaten, mocked and laughed at, simply because he maintained that he was who he was - the prince. I won't tell you the rest of the story, as you will enjoy reading the tale for yourself, but I will make use of it to make this point:

Despite what others say, and what circumstances surround you, once you have confessed Jesus Christ as your Lord and Saviour, and have believed it in your heart, you are a new creation; a child of God and a fellow heir with Christ himself. We need to become like the prince in the story, and become indignant with the thoughts that try to tell us otherwise. The young prince stamped his foot on the ground defiantly, and said, "I am the prince, and you have no right to be treating me this way." In his statement he was perfectly correct, and he knew it. As Christians we need to have the same amount of indignation and defiance towards things that are not the truth.
In our commercially oriented society, our advertising agencies and Hollywood

producers have made a lot of money brainwashing the general population into thinking what they should look like. Not only this, there is a general perception of what you should drive, what you should wear, the kind of house you should live in, how much you should earn, what you should drink, what sort of boyfriend or girlfriend you should have and so on. Unfortunately, the plastic soap opera image is very far from the many different kinds of people that are in the world today.
I mean the big hair, the plastic-surgery-generated faces and shapes, the clothes that are so impractical for mopping floors and gardening.
What in the world do they think ordinary people do?
But that is the plastic standard against which many people measure themselves. Is it any wonder that diseases like anorexia, bulimia and shop-o-holicism are running rampant in our society. Especially amongst the young people who often don't have the confidence to look different or wear anything different from what their peers are wearing.
But there are some things that not even money can buy, and so some people curl up under the enormous weight of having to accept that they are 'not good enough and never will be'. What else can they hide behind other than bad behaviour, or perfectionism?

There are all sorts of different lies that people believe about themselves:

Nobody loves me; everybody hates me;
May as well go and eat worms!
What use is it? There's no way I could ever be anything else!
I come from a long line of losers. I've always failed in the past;
I don't guess it'll change.
God loves perfection! How on earth could he ever love me?
If people really knew the real me, they would hate me!

Often these types of attitudes are a reflection of what we have heard as children. Our parents' words and attitudes often surface in the way we end up feeling about ourselves. We need to keep that in mind, particularly if we have children to influence!

Not only our parents, but also our teachers, peers and other relatives help shape our 'self-image'. It cannot be emphasised too strongly: we cannot base our decisions and actions upon the way we feel, even the way we feel about ourselves. They must be based on the truth of the Word of God. And so we come to the place where it's time to take off the mask of pretence, and to discard all the artificial props that we try to hide behind, and to offer up the real me to God our Father. The funny thing is, He knows exactly who we really are, and what we really look like, and has done all along - and He has loved us anyway! Perhaps He has thought we were funny, all done up in our man-made efforts to be somebody else - but still He loves us.

When it comes down to this point in our life, we should take a long, hard look at the frame of reference that influences the way we see ourselves. Below are two lists that outline the difference between man-made acceptance and worth and God bought acceptance and worth:

MAN'S ACCEPTANCE CRITERIA	GOD'S ACCEPTANCE CRITERIA
Who our earthly parents are	God's mercy and grace
What we look like	God's unfailing love for us
What kind of possesions we have	Our acceptance that God sent His Son
What kind of friends we have	Our acceptance of Jesus as our Savior
How often we go to church	Being set free from sin and death through the blood of Jesus Christ
How much we do for the Lord	God's having adopted us as children and fellow heirs
How rich are we	God's far-reaching forgiveness for all we have done.
How successful are we	

Do you have to look like a super model or an athletic sports star to be worth anything? No! Not unless you *are* a super model or a sports star!
Do you have to have several university degrees or be the Chief Executive Officer of a multi-million dollar business to be worth anything? No! Each vocational position, from garbage man to housewife, has its own value and worth, but even that is not the deciding factor as to a person's value or otherwise.

Do you have to have a totally clean slate, with no record of past misdeeds or crimes to be worth anything? No! Your value is wholly based on the love of God. The person who has been a prostitute, and the person who has won the Nobel Peace Prize are both equally in need of the grace of God, and this is given to both according to their faith, and even the faith is from God, it says in *Ephesians 2:8-10,* and leaves no room for anybody to think that he or she has done anything special. Read also *2 Corinthians 12:19 and Ephesians 3:14-21*

The long and the short of it is: every man and woman will stand before the throne of judgement, and our worth and acceptance on that day will be based entirely on the work of Jesus Christ and whether we have either accepted it or denied it. It has nothing whatever to do with any of Man's Acceptance Criteria. To improve the way you see yourself, study and memorise the Scriptures that tell you who you are in Christ, and the promises of what that means.
Ephesians 2:1-10; Colossians 2:13-15; 1John 2:28; 1John 3:1-2; 2 Corinthians 5:21; John 3:16; Romans 8:13-17
As you continually read the Word of God, and confess it, it will gradually wear away at some of the wrong perceptions that you have about yourself. In time, if you really desire it, you will have a revelation of what it means to be a child of God.
Remember, as in a family, the general peace and harmony between parent and child can be upset by certain behaviour, but there is nothing that can change the blood relationship that exists.

The father of a child will always be the father of that child, despite any communication or relationship breakdown that occurs.

It is the same with our Heavenly Father. Once we come under His salvation, we are His children, bought by His own blood. Nothing we have ever done, or even our seeming failures, can change that fact. There is nothing we can do to become more of a child of God than He has already done in the first place. Rather we should work at improving the state of our relationship with Him.

chapter eleven

PRIORITIES AND TOLERANCE LEVELS

Learning to cope in a crazy, mixed-up world

What a dramatic change has occurred in the way we live over the last hundred years. As a young person, I used to sit and listen to my grandmothers, as both of them would tell many stories of the 'olden days'. One grandmother, in particular, actually had the experience as a young girl of being a pioneer. Her parents, my great-grandparents, bundled their belongings on a bullock dray, tied a crate of chickens underneath, and the milking cow behind, and set off for a six week trek from Wirrabarra Forrest in the mid-north of South Australia, to an unsettled area not far from where Ceduna now is. Grandma was a young girl of about eleven at the time, and she and her sister walked most of the way. When they got there, there was absolutely nothing. They were among the first white settlers to ever make a home in the area. Everything they ate they produced themselves. All their entertainment was self generated - my grandmother told the story of their favourite game; one of the girls would climb a small tree, and the other would cut it down. It seemed like great sport, and it got the land cleared.

Communication with the rest of the world would have been next to nothing as they were isolated settlers, weeks away from any other settlement.

In her later years, I remember very well that she still held to a lot of her 'pioneer' type of practices. She made her own bread, kept her own chooks, and even though she lived in the town, she agisted a milking cow in a paddock not far away, and walked there every morning and evening to milk her. She grew her own fruit and vegetables, made her own jam and pickles, and took very cautiously to the new fangled innovations that technology brought her way. By the time she passed away in 1985, she had agreed to have an air conditioner, a television, and an electric stove, (they eventually removed the wood range oven). What a dramatic change from how she had lived as a child! Even her telephone was connected to an emergency dialling system, should she have an accident at home. Now, as a housekeeper, I don't have to boil my clothes in a copper and put them through a wringer; I don't have to beat the carpets as they hang over the clothes line; I don't have to go outside and cut the wood, to light the stove, to boil the water, to wash up the dishes; I don't have to empty ashes from the fireplace down the long-drop toilet; I don't have to pump the water, by hand, into a bucket to bring in for household use; I don't have to grow my own food in the garden, and preserve the excess for out of season use (though I still do at times); I don't have to clean and trim the kerosene lamps ready for use in the evenings, while my family amuses themselves with checkers or reading.

What a lot of labour saving devices have been invented, and how many of them do I use, including this word processor that saves my having to hand-write everything I think of? The microwave oven, the dishwasher, the automatic washing machine, the vacuum cleaner, the food processor, the supermarket grocery store, the restaurants and take-away food chains, the cheesecake shop, the gardening services. The list could go on and on and on.

Here's the crunch!

The more gadgets we have, and the more efficient our system of communication, travel and supply of goods, the more time we should have for rest and relaxation - right? In theory, one would expect that to be the case, but in practice, the common complaint of the new millennium is, "I just don't have the time!" Add to this, "I have so much to do, and I'm under so much pressure!"

"I have so much to do, and I'm under so much pressure!"

What is it about technology that has caused us to become a society of people who are highly prone to emotional and mental breakdown? Why are stress-related diseases top of the list as the ones most likely to cause failure of health? Why is it that mothers are unable to cope with two children, now with all the labour saving devices and child-care facilities, when in the past there were no such aids, and there were three to four times as many children? (My great-grandfather was one of twenty-two children. How on earth did his mother cope?)

In this chapter I would like to discuss several points that may give us some insight into this weird phenomenon, and hopefully will give us some different ways to begin to cope with the stress.

Read *Exodus 20:8-11*

This Scripture reference is actually the third of the Ten Commandments. 'Remember the Sabbath Day and keep it Holy' is the basic commandment, and then it goes on to outline exactly everything relevant to what that may mean.

Basically, it was a day of rest for the whole family, including the servants and the work animals. God handed this commandment down to Moses and made it one of the laws. Now the Ten Commandments were a summary of the whole law that was given to Moses, and it was always meant as a guideline for God's people to live by. It was always designed for the good of the people.

Over the thousands of years from then up to the time of Christ, the law became institutionalised and adapted to suit the religious leaders of that day. There were so many changes and amendments and sub-clauses added that it became almost impossible to deal with. The penalty for those Israelites who broke the law was fairly harsh, usually death. When Jesus Christ came, it was to set us free from the penalty of failing to keep the law, but that doesn't mean the law had no value, or has no value today. We still believe that it is wrong to murder, to steal and to lie.

We still believe that it is wrong to murder, to steal and to lie.

What about the law that commands we keep the Sabbath. Some Judeo/Christian expressions still hold firmly to Saturday as being the Sabbath day, as it was originally. It was Saturday that was the seventh day of the week, and was the day that God set aside as the day of rest. After the coming of Christ, the early church adopted another day, Sunday, as a day of celebration and gathering together to remember the death and resurrection of Christ. You will recall that Jesus rose from the dead on the first day of the week, Sunday. But as the early Christians were also Jewish, they still observed the day of rest on Saturday. That system went through a number of changes over the centuries until the last couple hundred years we saw a clear pattern emerge. We had in western Christian society a weekend. Saturday was like a business and family holiday, and Sunday was the day the family went to church to worship God and take communion. The church of the early twentieth century actually called Sunday, the Sabbath.
The question we have to ask here is, what day is the Sabbath actually, and are we breaking the Ten Commandments on a regular basis by not observing it as outlined in the law?

Read *Mark 2:24&27*
In this Scripture, Jesus had become involved in a disagreement with the Pharisees, who were the religious leaders of his time. They had accused him of not observing the Sabbath because he had healed somebody on that day.

Jesus' reply was that the Sabbath was made for man, not man for the Sabbath. Basically, He was saying that the principle of the Sabbath was given to mankind as a wise practice for our own good - the good of our health and the good of our family. But the Pharisees had made that law, and all of the law into a system of impossible rules and regulations that had become the master, instead of the servant. The Sabbath is for our use, not so that it controls us.

Sabbath is for our use, not so that it controls us.

Can you see how all principle of the Sabbath has been extracted from modern society? Some years ago, sport was introduced as a Sabbath event, and at first the church was very much against it. But gradually it accepted it as a matter of course. Then the retail industry pushed to have Saturday morning shopping, then Saturday afternoon trading, and then late night trading, and so on. In some states in Australia there has already been the push for twenty-four hour trading, including Saturday and Sunday. We have long since lost our day of rest, and Sunday is in grave danger of extinction as a day of rest or a day of worship. There are even a lot of tradesmen who now work on Sunday as a matter of course.

This is not good for society as a whole. We will only see an increase in stress levels, stress-related diseases and family breakdown because we have broken this simple commandment.

Does this mean that we should keep Saturday strictly as the Sabbath day of rest?

As Jesus said, the Sabbath is for man, not man for the Sabbath. Common sense tells us that, just as Jesus saw a need on the Sabbath and healed a man, so in our society there are the emergency services, which must work. Accidents tend to happen on any day of the week. Some babies are born on a Saturday. There are some things that need attention everyday of the week, so what are we to do? Well, the fact remains, we need a day of rest, whatever that day may be. Some people actually have to learn to take their day of rest, and not feel guilty about it. There are those whose value and worth has been based on their performance, who have got caught in the trap of work-a-holicism and who simply feel guilty to rest. This is not good: it is very bad. Your body was not designed by your Creator to work at this pace and period without the requisite amount of rest. That is why He gave the commandment in the first place.

Sometimes, I am unable to take a 'day' of rest, and so I take two half days, or

several quarter days. As a mother on demand, there are the busy times and the less busy times. I use the less busy times to put my feet up, read a book, and enjoy the sunshine - and I don't feel guilty about it, even if the dishes aren't done.
I would never be able to last the distance otherwise. I simply would be unable to cope.
Another commandment in *Exodus 20:17* is that of 'coveting your neighbour's goods'. Actually, it is the envy of your neighbour because he has a whole lot of things that you don't have.
Once again, this is not a law that was given to tie us up in knots, but to actually guide us into a freer life.

Envy of our neighbours' things - the old 'Keeping up with the Joneses' mentality.

It is this 'keeping up with the Joneses' kind of thinking that is driving society into a frenzied pace of activity, simply to support an unnecessary lifestyle. The advertising and retail industries are making millions out of the principle that people do envy other people's possessions, and will do almost anything to get them.
We must assess our real needs, and sort out the difference between them and our wants based on what we have seen everybody else doing and having. A growing family simply cannot keep up with the rate of fashion change that happens. You must surely have noticed: if it is stripes this year, it will be flowers next year, and spots the next, and then plain pastels, followed by browns and tweed. The problem is, the fashion change is usually so extreme that it is really noticeable if you are a season or two behind, and the peer pressure on those who fall behind the fashion is really very strong. You have to be completely indifferent to the opinions of others to ignore it, and merrily go ahead wearing your pleated tartan skirt of fifteen years ago. (Actually, if you still have one, hang onto it, as it will probably be back in fashion next year).

But fashion is not restricted to clothing. I have noticed it in relation to furniture, to cars, to house and garden, and the list goes on.

The fashion industry is not really concerned with how you look, or what your house looks like.

I mean, we've just been through the time where people rushed out to buy 'stressed' furniture; perfectly good furniture that had been deliberately scarred with hammers and chisels so that it looked old and worn out. How weird is that?

It is all about dollars and dollars (I was going to say cents, but nobody is interested in cents, only dollars!)
Sooner or later, as individuals under stress, we are going to have to make a stand in the face of this commercial pressure. We are going to have to learn to be content with the many good things that God has given to us, and resist the temptation to hanker after what we can't really afford, and don't really need!

Now, having just talked about the necessity of taking time to rest, it is appropriate to discuss the other side of the coin as well.

On the one hand we need a day of rest, and on the other, rest can be taken too far. We live in a society of wide extremes.

We see one sector of the community literally killing themselves and destroying their families because of an unhealthy addiction to work, and on the other extreme there are those that simply can't be bothered going to the employment office even to look for a job.

One is as bad as the other.
Balance seems to be the key word here. In *Proverbs 6:6* the Scripture paints the picture of the industrious ways of the ant, labouring hard all the summer in preparation for the winter. Here in the Proverbs it warns against sleeping when you should be working, as poverty will creep up upon such a person. The ant has a routine. It seems to know there is a time for work, and a time for rest. We also need to set a routine in our lives.

There is a time to wash, clean, shop, prepare food etc. There is a time to put domestic duties aside and focus on your children - their joys, disappointments, hopes and activities. There is a time to focus on other family members, though they should demand much less time than your immediate family. There is a time to gather with your spiritual family, at church. And there is a time for recreation. Recreation is important, but it should take its proper place and not encroach upon other responsibilities. Set everything in order, including your rest time. If domestic chores start to demand time set aside for your children, you should begin to look carefully at the situation. There are occasions when the housework is more than normal, say, when some disastrous bug has hit the house, and then you give more effort to the domestic chores.

But if it is continually stealing away from other important parts of your life, then you must prioritise. Sometimes you have to ignore a job you have been unable to finish.

Don't let the guilt of it eat you up and draw you away from your peace.

(I have written this principle in the context of a busy, at home mother, though the same principle applies to whatever area of life you happen to be employed in.)
Read *Proverbs 3:6; Colossians 3:23; Romans 12:1*

Sometimes we live under the misapprehension that the only way to worship the Lord is to be in church, with raised hands, singing praises to God. The above Scriptures indicate that we may worship the Lord with whatever we do. This must include cleaning the bathroom, scoring for the children's basketball game, keeping the front garden free of weeds, taking your grandmother to the doctor etc. In all things acknowledge Him and He will direct your paths. Yes! This is our spiritual service of worship.

This is our spiritual service of worship - it is the attitude with which we serve our responsibilities that is seen by the Lord, not necessarily how many church meetings we attend during a week.

Never forget that 'church' is a word that collectively describes those who have given their lives to Christ and are saved by Him. We live in a world full of responsibilities, and we must tend to them, making sure to take our day of rest and day of worship and celebration.
Read *Psalm 55:22; Psalm 37:1-11,23*

There are odd times in every life when it has all become too much. You have worked diligently; you have served faithfully, you have attended the gathering of the saints regularly; you have done everything you know to do, and now you have had it! Your body, your mind and your emotions are tired, and are telling you it is time for a rest. Now is the time to call an understanding friend or family member, arrange for them to have the children overnight, and take time to refresh yourself for just a few hours. If sound sleeping is what does the job, then do it. If going out to dinner with your spouse or friend will ease the strain, then do that. These are odd times, and you need to recognise the signs, because you know better than anyone just how little it will take to really lose the plot.

You must take the time out, perhaps twelve to twenty-four hours. The world won't fall apart while you drop out for a while, and when you are refreshed, you can get back to the business of responsibility with a renewed vigour and enthusiasm. Read *Luke 12:22-34; Matthew 6:34*

Possibly the best advice I ever heard was: 'Don't borrow trouble!

Don't borrow trouble!

That is exactly the essence of what Jesus was telling his followers in the gospels. 'Tomorrow will take care of itself. Each day has enough trouble of its own.'

There is just one small difficulty. When my grandmother was a girl, living with her family as pioneers on the west coast of South Australia, the trouble that she had to be concerned about involved that which was in her actual physical vicinity. She wasn't aware of the soldiers' dilemmas in South Africa as they fought the Boer War, neither did she have to worry about the philosophical debates that Charles Darwin was causing with his controversial theory of evolution. She didn't have to worry about the statistics of robbery, murder, assault, divorce, homelessness or any other statistic that reflected the state of her state's capital city. She would never have known about any of it. She probably didn't worry about the plight of the orphans in India, or the political tension in Europe. There was a very simple reason why these burdens didn't trouble her waking hours. She never heard about them. How could she? A bottle washed up on the sand would take as long to get there as it would take for the trouble to be over.

Our information highway - the high tech, satellite coverage of the world's tragedies - can have every worrisome bit of news in your lounge-room hours after the event has taken place.

If you choose, you can carry the burden of the whole world on your shoulders, as there are twenty-four-hour news channels that can tell you what you may or may not want to know. And the chances of it being good news are probably very small. I'm not suggesting we bury our head in the sand, but I am suggesting that as human beings, we were probably not created to carry the emotional burden of the whole world. Up until the introduction of television, and satellite communication, we probably managed to be aware of and pray for the troubles of our family, community, state, and sometimes nation, though that news would take a little longer to get to us.

Are you weighed down with concerns? Does the media coverage of the troubles in the Middle East cause you to intercede in prayer, or does it add another ulcer to your already suffering stomach. If you cannot hear about tragedy across the other side of the world without taking it as a worry to add to your life, then I suggest you stop watching news broadcasts, and start dealing with the issues that are immediately around about you. God is the Lord of heaven and earth. He commands that we be anxious for nothing, and not to worry, for it cannot add a single day to our life. In fact, scientists suggest that worry may be taking days off our life. To be informed should serve only to motivate us towards prayer on behalf of the suffering. It must not be as an added weight to our already troubled existence.

The world is a busy busy place, and we can become busy busy people, even in a lifestyle that has good as its aim. I have reached this conclusion: that in it all, God is the centre of all things, and as Paul states in *Philippians 4:6-9,* don't be anxious for anything, instead bring your needs before God, with thanksgiving, and fix your thoughts on all those things that are true, honourable, lovely, pure, right, excellent and praiseworthy. When you do these things, the peace of God, which surpasses all understanding, will guard your hearts and minds in Christ Jesus.

A FINAL WORD

In my thirty years of experience as a Christian (I gave my heart to the Lord when I was eight, so I'm not really that old) I have seen a lot of ideas, theories, practices and 'fads' come and go. Some have been really positive with great response and effect, and some I would rather not discuss. In it all, I have come to this conclusion - 'fads' come and go, but the Word of God stands true for all time.
In this last illustration, so wonderfully drawn by Ben Moulton, I have tried to capture an idea. With any new program or method that is introduced, each is proclaiming the latest 'miracle cure' for those life-long problems, and in most cases, there is great merit in the thoughts and theories offered. Particularly if the concept is recommending a deeper relationship with God, there is value to those who employ the suggestions. But with every new notion introduced over the last hundred years, there is always the danger of taking things too far.
In my illustration overleaf, you can see our character is in danger of his boat of life sinking in the sea of trouble, and he calls out for help to the Lord. He responds to the Lord's outstretched hand, and moves to the middle of his boat of life, and the boat steadies. But he soon spies something else, in the same direction to which he was moving, and goes past the stable influence of God, and into the extreme, where the boat is again unstable and he finally loses balance. As the little fish in the drawing exclaims -'Doh!'

In any theory or method that you hear about, move toward that which is backed firmly by the Word of God, but be careful of extremes. Sometimes the danger is in following a method, and putting it into the place of God Himself. It is not a method or a theory that brings you healing; it is God and comes through obedience to His Word.

I pray that you find a deeper relationship with our Lord and Saviour, and that you can trust Him enough to allow him to lead you through the valley of shadows and into His green pastures.

God Bless

Meredith Resce

GULP!
SPLASH!
BLIP... BLIP
THE BOAT TIPS TO ONE SIDE.
TIP!
HELP! THE BOATS GONNA TIP!
OH NO!
DON'T WORRY COME THIS WAY!
JESUS?
EH?
THE BOAT STEADIES...
IT IS YOU JESUS!
TIP!
YES!
HEY... I CAN FEEL LOVE FORCES HERE! YOU ARE A CHANNEL BABY... OM... OM. NEW AGE YEAH!
RAD!
FREAK!
THE BOAT TIPS!
C'MON TOUCH IT ... THE HEALING CRYSTAL!
WOW! WELL I NEVER.. WOOAH ... WOOAGH!
TIP
SPLASH
DOH!

notes

notes

notes

notes

notes

notes